BASIC
BODY REPAIR &
REFINISHING
FOR THE
WEEKEND MECHANIC
BY CARL CAIATI

TAB BOOKS Inc.
BLUE RIDGE SUMMIT, PA 17214

Other TAB Books by the Author

No. 1555 *Airbrushing*
No. 2112 *Customizing Your Van—2nd Edition*

To my dear sweet little Italian mother, who to this day wonders how I ever ended up working in a body shop.

FIRST EDITION

SECOND PRINTING

Printed in the United States of America

Library of Congress Cataloging in Publication Data

Caiati, Carl.
    Basic body repair & refinishing for the weekend
mechanic.

    Includes index.
    1. Automobiles—Bodies—Maintenance and repair—
Amateurs' manuals. I. Title. II. Title: Basic body
repair and refinishing for the weekend mechanic.
TL255.C24 1984   629.2'6'0288   83-24156
ISBN 0-8306-2122-9 (pbk.)

Cover illustration by Larry Selman.

Contents

Acknowledgments

It's nice to have friends; they read your books and give you a boost along the way. Mike Wright is not only a very good and reliable friend but also one of the best and most versatile body men in the business. Through his establishment, The Body Shop in Pompano Beach, Florida, have passed some of the vilest wrecks, coming out in virtually all cases as good as new. Mike was instrumental in laying out and doing the groundwork (and labor) on the wreck featured in the Laser Beam alignment material. Mike is one of the few Laser machine experts in the bodywork business and his efforts made the Laser beam treatise a unique presentation of this book, a feature of sophisticated body work made possible by the laser alignment technology instituted by Kansas Jack, Inc. With his expertise and complete knowledge of current and standard body shop techniques the name "Mike Wright" and term "Mike Right" have become synonymous in the field of quality body work. He also ably assisted in major advisory work in this simplified manual.

Peter J. Molinari deserves recognition for devoting a lifetime to impeccable body finishing and glorious paint work. Peter taught me (with much frustration to himself) the finer points of flawless surface preparation and painting. This wizard of the spraygun goes back to the early days of body painting—when the true craftsmen were not in danger of becoming extinct as they are today. Known as "The Hawk," Pete can spot any and every imperfection on a prepped car and helped greatly in improving my eyes even though they could never be equal to his, or as discerning.

Some of my co-workers at Collisions Specialists, Hollywood, Florida, also deserve mention as they proved to be not only good friends but eager assistants in some of the projects. Winston Peddlar, magnificent painter and prep man, served as cohort and model, as did Bert Henry.

My daughter Suzanne inadvertently aided his cause by smacking up her Mustang—giving me a dented fender to work on and use as an example.

My son Rick—"Mr. Fix-it" and a superb auto mechanic—assisted, advised, and donated his wrench-arm in a few situations.

Many of the fine representatives of leading equipment manufacturers also gave unstinting assistance and help with advice, technological material, and even equipment. This roster of valuable assistants includes Len Niese of BRUT Manufacturing Co.; Ed Miller, ad-sales manager of Chicago Pneumatic (Hennessy Ind., Inc.); Alice Rogers of Fibre Glass-Evercoat Co., Inc.; Ken Zino of Motor Magazine; and Willard L. Daluge of Seelye, Inc. I am particularly indebted to J.M. Bilderback of the advertising department of Linde (Union Carbide).

Introduction

Why do your own bodywork or paint repair? For the same reasons you paint or recarpet your house, repair your own appliances, upholstery, electrical gizmos, and so on.

For one thing, it's cheaper. With the high cost of living, it's to your advantage to become a weekend or part-time mechanic and serviceman. In many cases, insurance costs force you to carry a $200 deductible charge—which means that *you* pay the first $200 out of your pocket. This can be covered in radical repair damage situations; for the minor dents (which can also reach the $200 price tag) it means that you pay the major portion in a minor damage situation.

These same "minor damage" situations can be tackled successfully by anyone who can handle average home modifications and repairs.

Due to modern "miracle" plastic filling materials, quick-drying paints, and sophisticated repair and shaping tools, you can successfully and economically do your own small to average jobs. Bodywork need not entail years of training and expertise, as it once did. Filling in a crack or dent in an auto body need not be any more complex than spackling or contouring a piece of wood or plaster—provided that equal care is given the automotive project, coupled with study and practical application of the techniques involved. If damage is severe or excessive, you can always replace the damaged door, fender, hood, etc., with a new or used replacement part. In most cases, this is even easier than recontouring or refilling creases in the fractured metal.

This book is dedicated to the Mr. & Mrs. Fixit who are of average intelligence and budget minded to boot. Most of the work presented in this how-to manual can be done in a garage or driveway (weather permitting)—which virtually everyone has access to. You will learn basic techniques you can practice as well as recommendations as to what should be left to more sophisticated equipment and qualified personnel.

Study and read about a job before attempting it in all cases. Then do the job once—not twice or more because of poor planning or inferior application of tools and materials. Analyze the depth, extent, and solution to the problem and apply the correct procedure as detailed in this book. Bodywork will cost you a bit of time, but it can save you a lot of money.

Remember, good repair work keeps the value of your car up. Sometimes good body repair is as essential as a tune-up or lube job.

Keep in mind also that the work involved may be time-consuming but not demanding; it's as easy to do bodywork as it is to do engine work. Most repair jobs make excellent weekend projects that can be rewarding and fulfilling.

Important too is safety. Many body plastics, paints, liquids, and solvents are very toxic to the skin and hazardous to the human breathing apparatus. Religiously use protective eye gear, toxic vapor masks, and skin protection (gloves, etc.) in all instances that warrant them.

Safety equipment of all types is sold by the outlets that provide the products found in body shops. As part of your tooling and accessory roster, you should own eye protection (goggles or shield), a toxic particle mask, and a good strong pair of rubber gloves. Avoid skin contact with toxic solvents whenever possible.

I hope this introduction will instill some enthusiasm in you, and that you will nurture this enthusiasm into the energy necessary for application in basic bodywork.

Safety Precautions

Over the years, the ranks of automotive do-it-your-selfers have expanded to the point that almost all of us dabble in some sort of minor tune-up or overhaul work on a family or personal vehicle.

Auto body repair work, just as automotive mechanical work, can be tackled by the weekend do-it-yourselfer. Unlike mechanical work, which is basically assembly, disassembly, and bolt-on replacement work, bodywork necessitates a bit more care and expertise and, in many instances, increased labor time. The increased labor time however, is the one body shop factor where you, as a do-it-yourselfer, can realize the greatest monetary savings since the labor is applied by your own hands. You are trading time for money and in today's economy, the time trade is a more reasonable and tidier expenditure.

No doubt, bodywork needs a bit more than lay expertise, but the techniques and procedures can be easily mastered within a short time. The purpose of this book is to assist and enlighten the do-it-yourself enthusiast who wishes to repair, repaint, or even refurbish his own car or that of a friend, family member, or neighbor.

This book is not a body shop technician's manual;

some of the procedures and approaches are primitive and in some instances may seem crude. If they are very basic and employ very basic and seemingly obtuse tooling, they are laid out with budgetary considerations in mind. For instance, it is more professional and chic to utilize an air power expander to unbuckle a door, hood, or trunk in place of a 2×4 used as a lever — but how much cheaper and just as effective the 2×4 is!

Body shop repair tooling can be cheap and simple or expensive and sophisticated. Both extremes are presented within these pages. Most of the tooling mentioned should be the mainstay of the serious do-it-yourself bodywork enthusiast.

Safety precautions should be thoroughly covered and stressed, since some of the materials and tooling used in modern bodywork can be hazardous.

Always use a safety mask with proper filters to combat the toxic fumes and residue of acrylic lacquers, acrylic enamels, and all relating thinning mediums.

Some resins and body fillers may also be strong in odor and offensive to your lungs; if you find them contributing to lung discomfort use a mask with them as well.

When using auto body air tools, respect them as you would all hazardous cutting and grinding tools. When grinding and working with metal, always use goggles in conjunction with grinders, sanders, drills, air chisels, and cutters.

Protective face shields should always be used when sandblasting or gas welding. You can in no way successfully sandblast without eye protection, and flying sparks and popping metal create havoc with even the simplest welding job.

Many of the chemicals mentioned and recommended in this book may be skin irritants. When fiberglassing, use heavy cloth — or preferably — rubber gloves.

Refrain from putting or washing your hands in thinners; here too, use rubber or surgical gloves whenever possible. Resins and catalyzed media are highly irritant. Again use gloves, and if fumes get to you, use a mask.

Exercising and applying the basic procedures herein will enable even the neophyte to undertake and tackle home bodywork with successful and refined results.

Analyzing and Estimating Repair Work

Before making any repair job decisions you must first analyze and study the damage to the vehicle. You must ask yourself these questions:

- Is the damage worth fixing?
- Are the parts necessary available or within your budget?
- Is the repair work and expertise necessary within your skills?
- Can the job be undertaken with the basic materials and tooling described in this book?

Frame work and excessive structural damage should be left to the experts. They have the know-how and the heavy-duty equipment required to repair radical body damage situations. Figure 2-1 is a prime example of extensive body and structural damage that is out of the realm of the do-it-yourself novice. Here the doors have been severely crushed, and the door frame and structural post are completely wrecked. This case involves not only replacement of the doors but also re-straightening and realignment of the door post, frame, etc. Figure 2-2 shows the inner damage in the middle

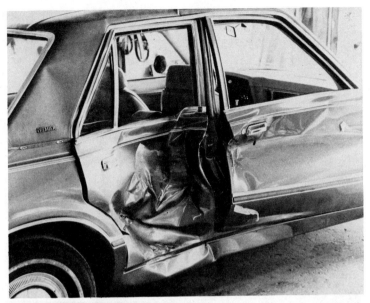

Fig. 2-1. A radical damage situation. Here the frame, doors, support post, and rocker panels are badly distorted.

stages of repair. The equipment being used is for heavy-duty frame alignment; it's very expensive and demands the expertise of an alignment specialist. When encountering extensive damage situations such as this one, it is best to seek the services of a qualified body shop or frame specialist.

To research needed repair parts and obtain their numbers, consult the *Motor* magazine crash manuals. These list every part of every car in handy, illustrated auto body part compendiums. This will aid you in ordering and guarantee that you will obtain the correct parts. The prices of all parts are listed, as well as time and labor factors involved so you can evaluate the cost of a major job that you may have to farm out to a commercial shop. *Motor* manuals are updated every year according to price changes and new vehicle additions.

Figures 2-3 through 2-9 show some typical minor-to-moderate body jobs that can be successfully undertaken by the average do-it-yourselfer or weekend mechanic.

Fig. 2-2. Repair work in the situation in Fig. 2-1 involves the use of heavy frame pulling and alignment machinery.

Fig. 2-3. This damage to hood and left fender is easy to repair, and involves simple hood and fender replacement.

6

Fig. 2-4. Here we need a front grille and header panel plus fender replacement. The twisted wheel will need a frame specialist.

Fig. 2-5. Dings such as this are common. A little filling and sanding and the ding will disappear.

Fig. 2-6. Front fender ding. Pulling the dent and smoothing it out with body filler will solve the problem.

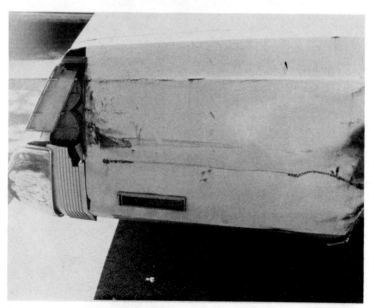

Fig. 2-7. Another practical do-it-yourself job involving basic body-work and taillight housing replacement.

Fig. 2-8. Here's a real easy one—a badly crushed door and door framework.

Fig. 2-9. The solution to Fig. 2-8 is replacement with a used door. The entire operation including repainting should take no more than three hours.

10

Basic Body Shop
Hand and Motor Tools

Proper and adequate tooling is the main prerequisite for refined bodywork. The old adage "a craftsman is only as good as his tools" applies in bodywork as in every craft endeavor.

Basic bodywork tooling is composed of both hand and machine tools. Usually the machine (air and electric) tools do the heavy work or rough finishing; the hand tools execute the finishing touches. In this chapter we will list and analyze the major tools needed by the do-it-yourselfer. You do not need to avail yourself of *all* the tools listed, only the ones you judge are suited to your purposes.

HAND TOOLS

Dent Pullers: These tools are a priority item; you cannot properly repair dents without some form of dent-pulling utensil. Figure 3-1 shows basic slide hammer pullers with their common attachments. The slide hammer has a screw nose that is screwed into a pre-drilled hole in dented sheet metal. The slide (H-handle) is then pulled toward the handle using combined weight and "pull power" to yank out the metal. The dent is

Fig. 3-1. Dent puller and related accessories. (courtesy Snap-On Tools)

usually pulled out in increments until the sheet metal is close to its original contour.

Figure 3-2 shows an available handy attachment (made by Mac Tools) that allows you to attach a pair

Fig. 3-2. Adaptor for retaining standard locking pliers is a handy accessory.

of locking pliers (such as Vise Grips) to the slide hammer nose. This slide hammer setup allows you to grab metal firmly in situations where the screw nose tip will not suffice (Fig. 3-3). Proper application of the slide hammer will be covered in Chapter 5.

A unique dent puller working on a leverage prin-

Fig. 3-3. The slide hammer/Vise Grip combo is ideal for pulling metal in awkward situations.

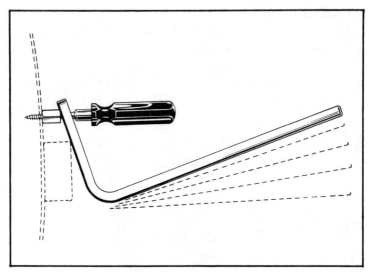

Fig. 3-4. A different method of dent pulling uses the leverage principle: the RB dent puller (courtesy R-B).

ciple but adequate in small dent situations is the RB puller (Fig. 3-4). Minor dents may also be pulled using the Lisle hand tongs (12150) shown in Fig. 3-5.

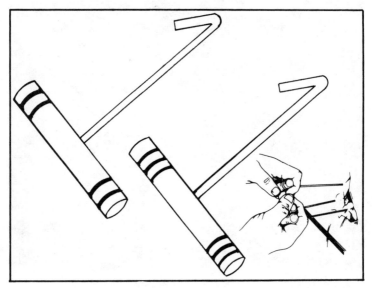

Fig. 3-5. Lisle dent pulling tongs are great for average dents.

Fig. 3-6. Bodywork hammers.

Body Hammers: Body hammers are specialized tools. They are not to be confused with the standard carpenter's hammer, which is not recommended for bodywork.

Body shop hammers are specifically designed for metal contouring (Fig. 3-6) and are used alone or with dollies (Fig. 3-7) to reshape metal. In the hammer-and-dolly method, the hammer strikes the shaping blow, while the dolly, acting as a mini-anvil held under the distorted metal section, aids in shaping. Dollies have curved or straight sides to conform to various contouring situations. When tapping down or straightening dents, light taps are used so as not to further distort the metal. In the *hammer-on-dolly* technique, the blow of the hammer must hit the crease directly over the dolly's surface. The hammer-on-dolly technique is used when

15

Fig. 3-7. A typical dolly.

the dent must be raised *above* the surface of the surrounding metal.

In the *hammer-off-dolly* technique, the dolly is placed under the metal but off the crease and adjacent to the hammer impact point. The dolly is placed off-center under the crease and light blows are struck around the peripheral areas of the crease. In this method, the distorted metal is struck *down* — the opposite of the hammer-on-dolly approach, in which the metal is forced *up*. Only areas raised above the original metal contour should be reworked, starting with the highest distortion point farthest from the central point of the crease. Again, tap lightly; excessive blows will cause newer and possibly worse dents.

Dollying out creases must be done with care and proper hammer and dolly coordination, which is attained by practice and experience. Dent straightening can also be achieved using the hammer in conjunction with the slide hammer. (Again, Chapter 5 explains dent manipulation.)

"Cheese Grater" Files: These are used for rough shaping of freshly plastic-filled areas prior to fine finish sanding

(Fig. 3-8). They cut down body filler quickly and efficiently (see Chapter 5). The smaller hand files allow access to sharp and close contoured areas; the long file is used for general large area forming.

Straight-Line Hand Board: Also known as the *straight board*, the *long board*, and (facetiously) as the "idiot stick," this is a hand tool that functions as the straight line air sander — more controllable and slower but more exacting for achieving correct, accurate large area body

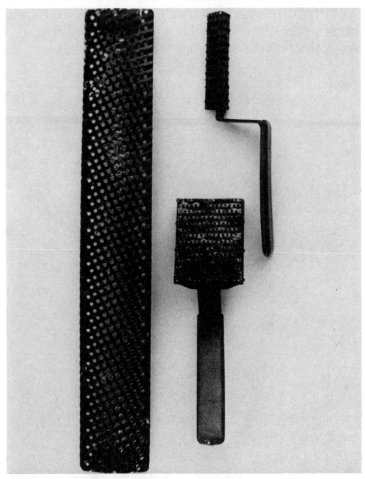

Fig. 3-8. "Cheese grater" files.

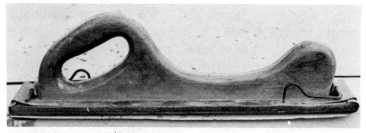

Fig. 3-9. Straight line hand sander.

contouring. It is used in conjunction with grades of sandpaper from 36 to 180-grit in a special size formulated for use with this tool. The sandpaper strips are retained by pressure clips; this allows quick-change capability when the sandpaper is worn (Fig. 3-9).

Sanding Block. This is a smaller rubber straight block that

Fig. 3-10. The hand sanding block is used in situations where the straight board is too awkward.

is handy for contouring confined areas not accessible with the long board (Fig. 3-10).

Sandpaper: Sandpaper is not so much a tool as an accessory to be used with sanding boards, blocks, air tools, and the hand itself. Sandpaper is marketed in various shapes and sizes to be used with corresponding tools (Fig. 3-11). The grits you will be most concerned with are:

- *36-grit* for body filler contouring or sanding paint down to bare metal.

Fig. 3-11. Sandpaper types available for different tools and hand sanding (sheets).

Fig. 3-12. The squeegee.

- *80* to *100-grit* for finer finishing of plastic or rough finishing puttied or primed areas.
- *220* and *320-grit* for sanding and feathering surfaces to be painted.
- *400* and *600-grit (wet)* for final surface finishing prior to buffing.

Squeegee: This is the basic applicator for applying body filler, putty, etc., (Fig. 3-12). Squeegees come in a variety of sizes.

MACHINE TOOLS
In this category are included essential machine tools; these are virtually all air types and must be powered by means of an air compressor (minimum 1½ horsepower).

Air Drill: Always a body shop mainstay, the air drill may be replaced by the household standby electric drill.

Air drills will handle light or heavy-duty drilling jobs including frame drilling or accessory and parts installation (Fig. 3-13). Air drills are preferable to electric drills, and offer some distinct advantages: air drills do not overload, stall, or burn out since they generate less heat and contain no brushes or armatures to wear out. Air drills are also smaller and lighter in weight, hence easier to manipulate.

Air Wrenches: An air ratchet is not mandatory for body and assembly work, but it is much less tedious to use than hand wrenches. The air ratchet can be a time-saving and effective tool applicable to all wrenching operations (Fig. 3-14).

Straight Line Air Sander: The straight line sander, a basic body shop tool, is great for large area contouring and leveling. Straight line sanders are primarily intended to cut body fillers (Bondo, fiberglass, etc.) and some will accept conventional metal cutting files for working on metal. Delivering 3000 strokes per minute, the straight line air sander will accept the same sizes

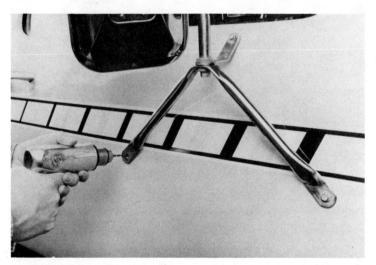

Fig. 3-13. The air drill in use, mounting a mirror.(courtesy Chicago Pneumatic)

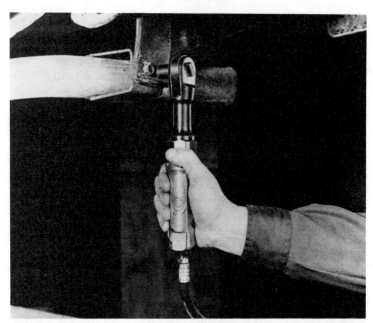

Fig. 3-14. Bolt removal with the CP828 ⅜ heavy-duty ratchet wrench.

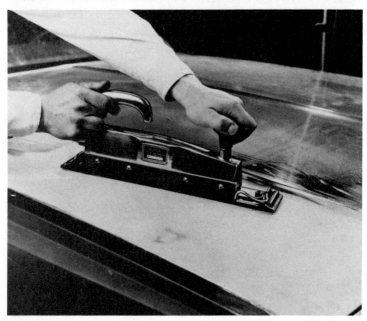

Fig. 3-15. A typical situation involving the straight line sander. (courtesy Chicago Pneumatic)

and grades of sandpaper as the hand-operated straight line long board. Figure 3-15 shows a typical straight line air file in operation.

Dual-Orbital Sander: Commonly referred to in body shop terminology as the *DA*, rotary-only or random orbital actions are provided with this revolving air sander (Fig. 3-16). In straight rotary mode, the DA works well to grind down body fillers or remove old paint from metal surfaces. In random orbital (eccentric rotation) mode, the DA provides finer finishing than disk or straight line units. The off-center motion assists in keeping the abrasive disks used free of paint films that can clog sandpaper and hinder cutting action. A built-in speed regulator allows matching of the tool's speed to specific jobs. Circular backing pads for the DA are available in five-and six-inch diameters; the most common and preferable is the five-inch pad. Pressure-stick sanding disks in grit sizes from 36 to 360 are marketed for use with the highly efficient DA.

Jitterbug: Another orbital-type finishing tool, but more

Fig. 3-16. The CPA 864 Random Orbital Sander. (courtesy Chicago Pneumatic)

Fig. 3-17. The "Jitterbug" (Model CP 766). (courtesy Chicago Pneumatic)

applicable for fine-finishing straight or level surfaces, the jitterbug fits the palm of the hand and is easily manipulated. It offers precise control for smoothing and blending fillers and fine-feathering paint repair areas. This sanding unit is ideal for preparing prepainted surfaces needing fine sanding in order to sufficiently grip primer or paint overcoats (Fig. 3-17).

Air Chisel or Hammer: A handy and useful tool, the air chisel will greatly assist in a variety of body shop jobs. The key to this tool's versatility is the large selection of cutters and impact tips available. The air chisel can be used for splitting fasteners, driving bushings, splitting spot welds, and cutting sheet metal rapidly and efficiently (Fig. 3-18).

Polishers: Actually grinders with special adapters for polishing (Fig. 3-19), these units are necessary for buffing and fine-finish polishing of lacquered and enameled surfaces. They are used with buffing and polishing bonnets and rubbing compounds and polishes in order to obtain a glasslike finish.

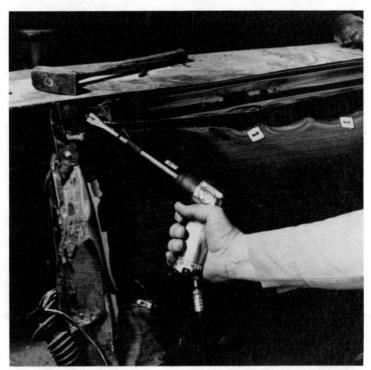

Fig. 3-18. The air chisel in use, cutting away retainers. (courtesy Chicago Pneumatic)

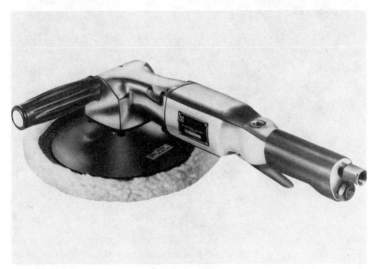

Fig. 3-19. CP 869S Air Polisher. (courtesy Chicago Pneumatic)

Sandblasters: Heavy-duty air tools, sandblasters are highly recommended. They are superior for removing and eliminating rust, stripping paint, and etching metal. A sandblaster is a well-recommended investment since

Fig. 3-20. The finest all-around sandblaster for the do-it-yourselfer and pro alike—the Brut Model 70S. Its specially designed nozzle makes this one of the most flexibly efficient units available.

it has a wide range of uses in body shop and household applications alike. After the initial investment, the sandblaster is cheap to operate and will last a lifetime with no breakdown problems. A good basic unit is shown in Fig. 3-20. Its application is demonstrated in Chapter 14.

Air Compressor: If you are serious about bodywork, you need a good, reliable air compressor. One can be purchased outright or they can be rented for a reasonable price. For body and paint work a 1½-, 2-, or 3-horsepower compressor is adequate; the 3-horse is the most efficient, but also the most expensive to purchase or rent.

Body Filler Repair Materials

Decades ago, refining and filling dents, creases, and general metal damage was undertaken with much hand labor. The filling medium then used to fill in and contour wrinkled metal was lead, which had to be melted down and puddled into recesses while heat was applied and then ground down by machine and hand. The process was costly (especially in terms of labor applied) and was mostly left to the resources of bona-fide expert body men. It was not a job for the average do-it-yourselfer with limited time and expertise. Though the lead filling procedures were radical, they are still considered today to be most effective and superior, though on a practical level virtually obsolete. Where leadwork is still available, costs involved are, if not prohibitive, out of line with today's improved body surface refining procedures.

The body fillers of today (and there are various types for specialized application) consist of plastic and resin mediums. The plastic-type agents — which are basically the thicker substances that must be mixed with a catalyzing and hardening creme — are designed for bodywork finishing and filling of metal. Some specially formulated types are intended specifically for fiberglass filling on damaged surface areas and cracks. The true liquified resins (which also must be catalyzed) are more widely used for fiberglass work in conjunction with fiberglass cloth. These resins are slower-drying and their bulk filling properties can be limited unless additive filler agents are available for these systems.

To familiarize you with the different forms of modern filling and refinishing materials, I have listed in this chapter the most commonly available items and their applications and functions.

"Bondo"

Bondo was originally the brand name of one of the earliest body plastics but the name is often used incorrectly as an almost generic reference to this distinctive type of body filler, which is used throughout the auto body industry. I will refer to it throughout this book as *body plastic*, which it is also commonly called.

Body plastic is a very viscous substance, almost the firmness of clay but much more malleable. Virtually all body plastic materials marketed today come packaged in cans of from one quart to five gallons. Quart cans are ideal for small jobs, the gallon cans are suited for larger (area) applications. In some cases, a gallon will suffice to do an entire car with average damage. The larger five-gallon bulk packaging is strictly for the professional body shop.

To obtain a proper working solution, the body plastic material must be catalyzed. Included with each can of body plastic is a hardening agent or creme that must be thoroughly mixed into the plastic material prior to its application. The working solution *must* be properly and adequately mixed according to the manufacturer's stipulations, which must be adhered to religiously.

The procedure is fairly simple. First the bulk filler should be thoroughly mixed. If the solution in the can has been left standing on the dealer's shelf, the liquid content may separate and flow to the top of the can. (This condition can be readily discerned when the can is opened.) Stir the filler vigorously and thoroughly until the liquid matter is fully absorbed by the filler and the solution attains a pasty appearance.

To mix a working solution, scoop up the required amount and add as much creme hardener as specified on the can label. Mix in the hardener (which is a different color than the filler stock) with a swirling, back-and-forth lacing-in motion until the solution is fully uniform in color. A good mixing tool is the flat squeegee, which is used in a back-and-forth lapping motion on a mixing board, working the hardener rapidly into the filler. Remember to adhere precisely to the manufacturer's recommendations. Pick up the filler mass and turn it over continuously with firm, even motions. This will help prevent the formation of air pockets and bubbles that can consequently cause pinholes in the filler's surface when it hardens.

A few other basics should be kept in mind. Mix the filler-hardener solution on a nonporous and clean surface (metal is best) or you may have adhesion problems. A plastic mixing board will also serve well; avoid cardboard, as the waterproofing waxes applied to cardboard can intermix with and affect the filler in the mixing process.

Avoid using excessive hardener; it doesn't accelerate the setting action by much nor does it make the solution harder. Excessive hardener can cause pinholes and poor bonding due to an overactive chemical reaction between the filler and catalyst.

Insufficient hardener can also work adversely, causing blistering and peeling when the contoured plastic is later feather-edged and primed. The color change in the filler after the hardening agent is introduced should be significant, but not overly pale or overly prominent. Experimentation is strongly recommended; this can be undertaken with small quantities to familiarize you with the physical changes that manifest themselves in body filler mixing with differing filler-to-hardener ratios. Keep in mind that body plastic sets up quickly, so it must be applied as soon as it is thoroughly mixed.

Many body plastics in all price ranges are available at your neighborhood body shop supplier. Ultra-cheap body fillers are not recommended. One of the better products is produced by Fibre Glass Evercoat, Inc. (Fig. 4-1). Quality body plastics also to be recommended

Fig. 4-1. Super White Star is one of the favored "Bondo"-type mediums.

are Marson White fill, Ditzler Ditz-Flex, and the ever-popular Bondo.

"METAL" BODY FILLERS

These, although referred to as "metal" body fillers, are in reality plastic fillers that are heavily saturated with metal (usually aluminum) filler material. The so-called "metal" body fillers are preferred over standard body fillers in situations when high resistance to moisture is required. For this reason, the "metal" fillers such as Pure Metal, Alum-a-Lead, and All-Metal are generally most applicable to situations involving rust damage and excessive moisture damage, as they are less porous

Fig. 4-2. Pure Metal is a better filler type for rust repair situations.

than standard types and so more resistant to humidity and moisture.

The product in this group I would most enthusiastically recommend to the do-it-yourselfer is Evercoat Pure Metal, which can be purchased in quart and gallon sizes (Fig. 4-2). Pure Metal is an aluminum-filled medium that is rustproof and waterproof. This filler is ideal for overcoating welds and welded-on patches. It is excellent in rust work and rust hole patching, adhering firmly to metal surfaces. It does not pinhole as much as standard body plastic, and is stronger to boot. It does not sand as easily as standard filler, but can be shaved and worked over easily in its early hardened stage, providing above-average durability and good featheredging.

Pure Metal is mixed in the manner of standard fillers — a creme catalyst must be worked into the bulk solution. It is applied preferably with a squeegee (as body plastic); after it has set it may be shaved, sanded, and overcoated with primer. For rust work, Pure Metal is far superior to standard fillers — and in most cases, costlier. Considering its advantages, though, it is an indispensible material for rust prevention and repair.

FIBERGLASS BODY FILLERS

Many body fillers on the market are particularly useful for work on fiberglass (Corvettes and similar special body types). They are not resins, but are more closely related to standard body plastics. Not as resilient as the "metal fillers," they are nonetheless stronger than standard body plastics in some instances as well as somewhat more moisture-resistant. These materials contain heavy fiberglass fiber content throughout, serving as filler additive. Most fiberglass fillers use a hardening agent similar to standard body plastics and are quick-setting.

Some of the leading fiberglass fillers including Tiger Hair, Evercoat's 'Vette Panel Adhesive/Filler

Fig. 4-3. Vette fiberglass filler.

(Fig. 4-3), and Marson's Stuff-It (Fig. 4-4). Another product specifically formulated for Corvette panel filling is Eckler's R-914.

Fiberglass fillers can be used for rust patching but are not (in my opinion) as efficient as metal-impregnated fillers. Fiberglass fillers rely on creme hardeners (benzoyl peroxide) for catalyzation; in many instances liquid hardener (methyl-ethyl-ketone peroxide) may be substituted. The use of creme hardener is recommended for the laymen; it is easier, automatically "color coding" the mixing ratios.

Fig. 4-4. Stuff-It fiber reinforced filler.

FIBERGLASS RESINS

Fiberglass resins are more universally applied in marine work (Fig. 4-5) but identical materials can be utilized effectively in auto body fiberglass repair and rust work. Resins used with fiberglass cloth will effectively repair and strengthen header panels and other similar fiberglass molded components. The resin-and-cloth method will also patch rust holes, offering optimum moisture resistance. The only negative factors with fiberglass resins are slow drying (setup) times and lack of bulk and malleability, as resin is a free-flowing liquid that

Fig. 4-5. Fiberglass resin is available everywhere and is used with fiberglass cloth.

is retained mainly by the fiberglass cloth that it must be used with. It is harder to sand than conventional body fillers, but consequently stronger. Fiberglass powder fillers may be added to the liquid resin to create a paste medium, but prolonged setting-up time makes resin second choice to conventional fillers. Body plastics set in minutes; with resins, it's usually a matter of hours. Resin thickness must also be built up slowly and in stages, involving unfavorable labor and waiting time.

For fiberglass and Corvette repairs, however, resins

are irreplaceable; use the resin-impregnated cloth procedure for strengthening and reinforcing damaged fiberglass areas as shown in Chapter 16.

Fiberglass resin is catalyzed with liquid methyl-ethyl-ketone peroxide according to the manufacturer's recommendations. Resin is extremely messy to work with, as well as highly toxic, so use it with caution. Most of the body materials in this chapter are skin irritants, so use care and protective rubber gloves in all instances. Body plastics and resins create havoc with manicures; try to avoid skin contact as much as possible. Avoid inhalation of all body plastic and resin fumes; use them only where optimum ventilation exists.

GLAZING PUTTY

Glazing putties are filling media but in no way apply to bodywork filling. Their specific purpose is to fill in scratches in primed surfaces and paint films. Glazing putty is skimmed on and when properly applied offers surface film coverage slightly thicker than primer coatings. Less viscous than body filler but denser than paint, putty must be administered over a paint or primer coat; never over bare metal. Glazing putty is best applied with a squeegee tightly and evenly over the scratched or chipped area to be smoothed out. It must be allowed to dry at least one hour, after which it may be sanded smooth until scratches are evened out and feathered in. If scratches still appear consecutive coats of putty should be applied and sanded down until all surface imperfections are eliminated.

Glazing putties are available from auto finish suppliers. Standard brands include Ditzler, 3-M, and Nitro Stan.

A newly released putty from Fibre Glass Evercoat (Fig. 4-6) offers some unique new advantages. This newest ultra-smooth polyester glazing medium can be applied over body fillers, metal or fiberglass, primer, or old sanded finishes. Its distinct advantages over

Fig. 4-6. Evercoat catalyzed glazing putty.

conventional putties include less shrinkage, quick drying, and capability for filling in rust-pitted areas following grinding or sandblasting.

Evercoat glazing medium is a two-part solution working on the same principle as body fillers. Evercoat must be applied in thin coats, overall coats not to exceed a thickness of ⅛ inch.

Since glazing putties are used as prepping media prior to painting, their proper administration will be presented in Chapter 18.

Basic Bodywork Primer

The greater part of the weekend mechanic's bodywork will involve applying and contouring body fillers. This is the approved method for patching and eliminating the minor dents and dings that the neophyte is most willing and apt to tackle.

This chapter presents pictorially three typical basic filling and contouring approaches. The first approach, on a van door, treats the simplest refinement task — filling in over a straight line area. The second job involves achieving a convex contour on a wrinkled fender. The third study involves rounding off a corner, a more complex task.

Figures 5-1 through 5-11 show how straight line contouring is achieved.

The second example is a basic wrinkled fender on a 1975 Mustang. Figures 5-12 through 5-22 show the proper refurbishing approach for this type of damage.

The third case is a more complex situation. The dent must not only be filled in but rounded out exactingly. Figures 5-23 through 5-28 show how this is brought about.

The three examples illustrated are the most simple

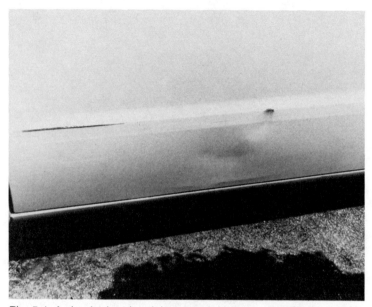

Fig. 5-1. A simple dent involving a straight line contouring situation.

and common types of problem you are likely to encounter. You can easily handle these jobs with minimal expenditures and basic knowledge and tooling.

Fig. 5-2. Holes are drilled to allow application of the slide hammer.

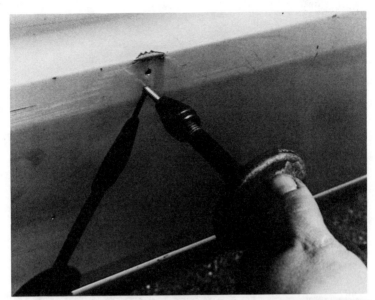

Fig. 5-3. The slide hammer point is screwed into the access hole on the top crease and the dings are pulled by slamming the counterweight back against the slide hammer handle. With minor dent damage such as this, the counterweight action should be moderate. Don't over-pull.

Fig. 5-4. The next crease in the panel is pulled in the same manner as the first.

Fig. 5-5. The entire area to be filled is ground down. A DA with 80-grit disk will get you down to bare metal quickly.

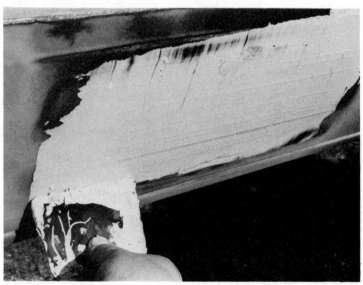

Fig. 5-6. Body filler is catalyzed and mixed thoroughly, then applied as evenly as possible with a plastic squeegee.

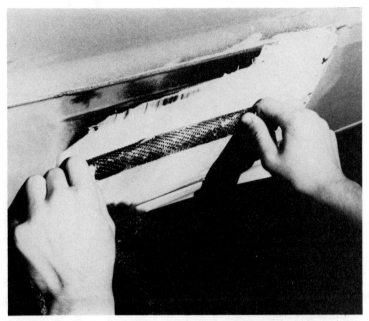

Fig. 5-7. The area is roughly contoured with a "cheese grater" file.

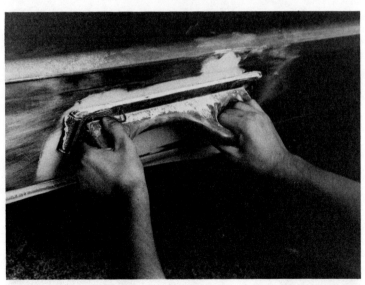

Fig. 5-8. Now the straight line sander or longboard is brought into play. Sand up and down, then in diagonal left and diagonal right directions. This will aid in achieving a straight, even surface. Sandpaper applicable here is 36-grit.

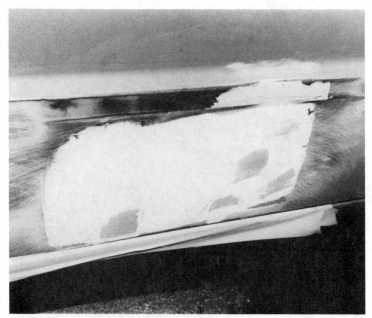

Fig. 5-9. If low spots occur, they will need to be filled again.

Fig. 5-10. After a perfectly straight, smooth patch is achieved, the area is primed, then puttied as shown to fill in sanding scratches.

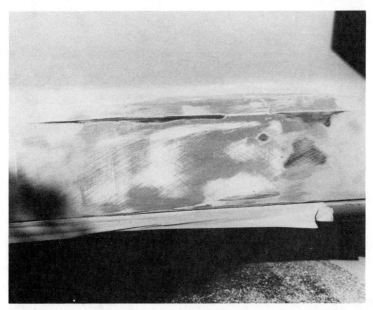

Fig. 5-11. The area is then finish-sanded with the long board and 100 grit sandpaper. The patched area is now ready for final priming and painting.

Fig. 5-12. A more prominent crease is exhibited in this damage to a 1975 Mustang involving fender panel and chrome molding.

Fig. 5-13. The chrome molding is removed and straightened by bending it back to shape over a block of wood.

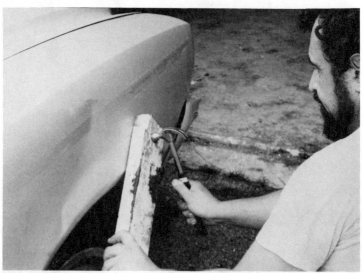

Fig. 5-14. The prominent outward kink is hammered back close to original contour using a hammer and 2x4. The 2x4 prevents hammer ding damage that may further distort the metal.

Fig. 5-15. Drill access holes, then apply the dent puller as necessary to pull out dents.

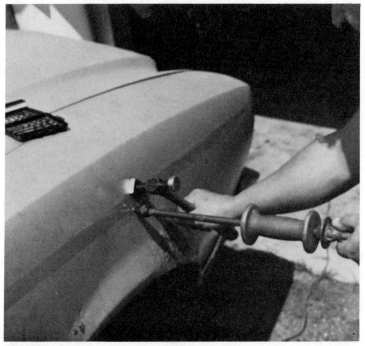

Fig. 5-16. Combined use of puller to pull and hammer to reshape is another approved and effective method.

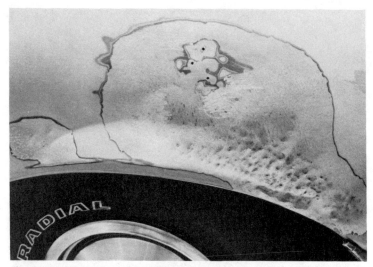

Fig. 5-17. After the metal is brought back close to its original contour with puller and hammer, it is ground down with a grinder or DA.

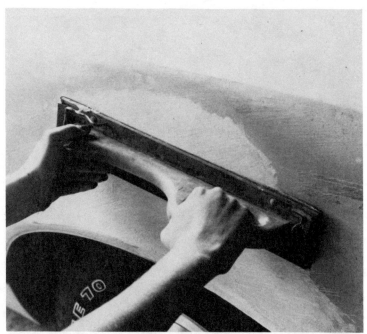

Fig. 5-18. Body filler is applied and rough contoured with a cheese grater file. Now the long board with 36-grit paper is brought into play. Follow the contours of the fender areas immediately adjacent to the damaged area.

Fig. 5-19. For out-of-the-way or tight, round contour areas inaccessible to the long board, the small block can be utilized.

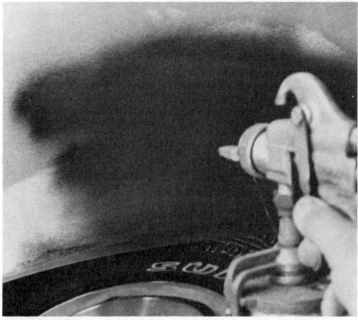

Fig. 5-20. When the plastic work is finished, prime the plastic and peripheral area.

Fig. 5-21. Putty to fill in minor waves and scratches, then reprime and paint.

Fig. 5-22. The finished repaired fender. With care and patience in applying fillers, the dent can look like new with patchwork undiscernable.

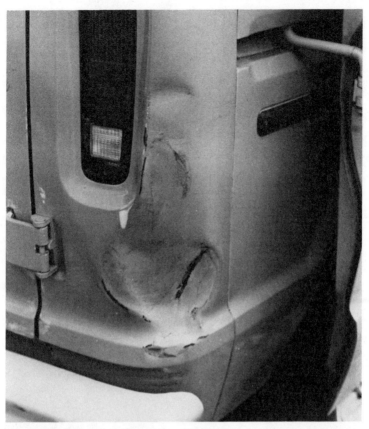

Fig. 5-23. More complex dents are those involving exacting contouring such as on the rear of this van. After filling, body lines must be brought back to their proper perspective.

Fig. 5-24. The metal is first pulled out as described in the first two examples. Hammer work may also be necessary. Then the area is ground down to bare metal for proper filler-to-metal adhesion. A hand grinder is used to get into the deep ruts.

Fig. 5-25. Ready for filler. Notice how most of the damaged metal has been worked up close to the original contours with slide and body hammer. The less filler that must be applied, the better and easier the final results.

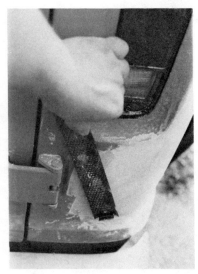

Fig. 5-26. After building up with body filler, the corner must not only be smoothed but shaped as well. A number of applications of filler may be necessary before the proper contour is achieved.

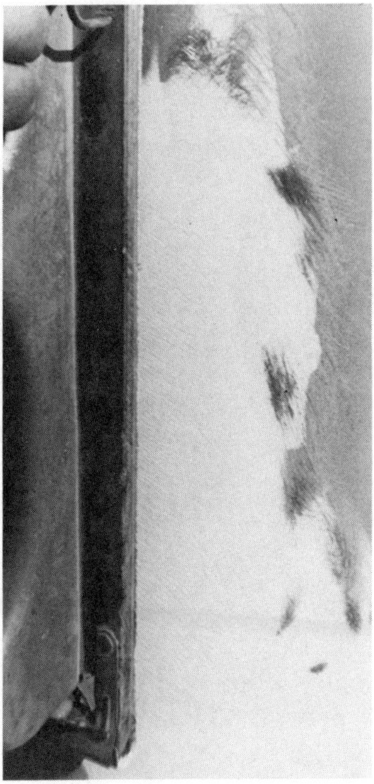

Fig. 5-27. The long board with 36-grit sandpaper is used in a horizontal motion around the corner until roundness is precise.

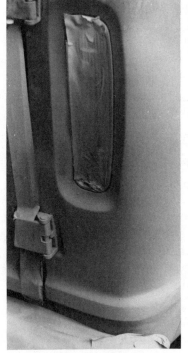

Fig. 5-28. As in the previous example, when shaping is complete, the area is primed, puttied, sanded with 100-grit paper and long board, and re-primed. Shown here is the repair up to its second priming stage. It is now ready for final painting.

Final Surface Finishing

There is a period between applying and shaping body filler and the final painting that is critical and governs how smooth and flawless the final paint coat will be.

Working the plastic surface with the handboard and 36 to 80-grit sandpaper will leave many deep, prominent scratches. These scratches should be minimized and the edges of the patched area feathered into either the metal or painted substratum. Sanding and feathering at this stage is best done using a jitterbug flat vibrating sander as shown in Fig. 6-1. The best grades of sandpaper to use here are 100 or 120-grit dry. After the surface is as smooth as possible through jitterbug sanding (Fig. 6-2), it should be primed. Use a good grey primer (acrylic type) such as Ditzler Primer 32 or other brand-name equivalent. The working area should be built up with heavy consecutive coats of primer (mixed one part primer to one part thinner), sanding between coats until all scratch traces have been removed.

Priming is also recommended over pre-painted surfaces or finishes in order to promote a good bond between old and new paint films as well as to fill in surface nicks and abrasions.

In cases of bodywork where excessively deep scratches (from heavy 36-grit final sanding) prevail, the use of spot putty is advised prior to priming. Spot or glazing putty is a very viscous medium with filling properties far superior to primer. It is too dense for spray application and must be applied with the squeegee. The squeegee is dipped into the putty (or putty is

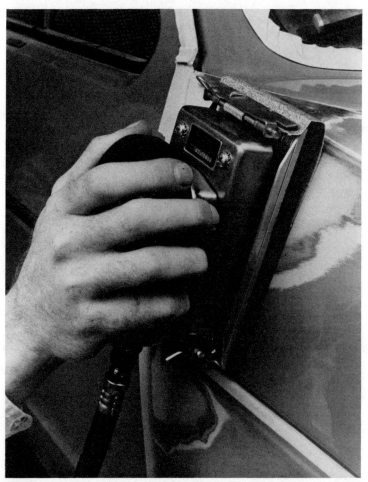

Fig. 6-1. The Jitterbug is a most efficient tool for smoothing and sanding surfaces (courtesy Chicago Pneumatic).

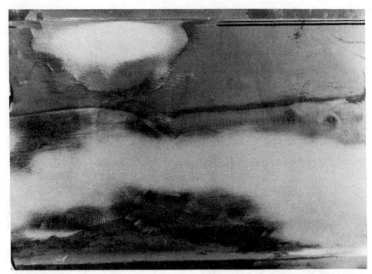

Fig. 6-2. Body filler properly surface-finished and ready for the initial primer coat.

applied to the squeegee as necessary with tube-type putties), then a skim coat is applied by squeegeeing the putty onto the surface (Fig. 6-3). The putty should be evenly applied all over the bodywork surface *after* it

Fig. 6-3. Putty is best applied with a plastic squeegee.

Fig. 6-4. The long board with 100-to 120-grit sandpaper is used to smooth out puttied surfaces.

has been given one full coat of prime. After the putty has been allowed to dry for a few hours, it is sanded and blocked out with a long board (Fig. 6-4), or with a small block in more confined areas. Figure 6-5 shows

Fig. 6-5. A smoothed-out and featured putty coat ready for topcoat priming.

a blocked-out puttied area ready for priming again. At this point the necessary prime coats to finish the surface and ready it for paint can be applied to cover minor sanding scratches. The best sanding grit to use for blocking-out putty is 120. It cuts through the putty quickly and leaves only minor surface scratches that cover easily and well with two or three heavy coats of primer.

Once the repaired area is primed, puttied, sanded, reprimed, and resanded, it is ready for painting. To perfectly smooth out the final coat or primer (prior to painting), use 220 or (better yet) 320 dry sandpaper.

Welding Metal

There are two basic types of welding used on metal: *gas welding* and *arc welding*. Both are qualified methods; they differ basically in mode of operation and versatility. In a number of areas they overlap in the types of work applicable.

GAS (OXYACETYLENE) WELDING

The oxyacetylene welding system comprises a torch with interchangeable cutting and brazing tips. The cutting tip is strictly for cutting sheet or solid metal or for high heat application. The brazing (welding) tip is mainly used for fusion welding of steel or brazing with brass. A very hot flame, fed by an acetylene and oxygen mixture regulated by controls on the torch handle, is the means by which metals are fused and untied, usually with the aid of steel or brass welding rod.

ARC (ELECTRIC) WELDING

In arc welding, an electric current is used to create a high-temperature "arc" between the welding rod and metal pieces to be joined. Instead of the torch is a handle that houses the welding rod; this rod serves as the electrode in the arc circuit. A generator provides arc voltage that may be varied depending on the density and thickness of the metal.

Arc welding is generally confined to the heavier-duty body shop work, usually on frames and structural components where pinpointed heat concentration is crucial in order to avoid damaging the molecular structure of some of the more exotic metals. These may become weakened when exposed to the high and widespread heat of an oxyacetylene torch.

Since the do-it-yourselfer should be steered away from the heavy-duty work, I will confine this welding primer to simple brazing techniques that the average neophyte can use and that are within the scope of the Saturday mechanic. The welding recommended and undertaken in this book will be confined to simple brazing—mainly patchwork on a small scale with thinner metals. Rust work patching will be discussed and explained. Since the patched rust areas will be overcoated with a metal-impregnated body filler medium, you need not concern yourself with exotic, perfect welds. If you follow these instructions, you can produce good if not perfect brazing.

Oxyacetylene torches and gas tanks are readily available on a rental basis and this is an economical and sound route to take.

HOW TO WELD WITH OXYACETYLENE

The preliminary steps involve hooking up the apparatus. Oxygen and acetylene gas bottle should always be stored and set up in a vertical position, and such that the acetylene and oxygen cylinder valves face away from each other. After the safety caps are removed, the regulators and gauges should be attached to their respective cylinders. Now the hoses are attached. The hose for the acetylene is colored red with its own "hex split" fitting containing a left-hand thread. The oxygen hose is green with fittings that are right-handed. The opposite ends of the hoses are attached to the torch or torch body. Threads are properly keyed, as are the torch values.

Now the torch can be set up for brazing. Make sure the valves on the torch are shut down, then open the air tank valves and set the gas pressures. For thinner metals (1/64″ to 1/16″), oxygen acetylene pressure should be 1 psi. Heavier sheet metals (up to 1/8″) will require a 2 to 3 psi setting for each gas. At this time check for leaks at all fitting points using soapy water. If all checks out safely, you are ready to ignite the torch.

The regulator valve at the acetylene tank should be open about one and a half turns, the valve at the oxygen tank all the way. The acetylene torch valve is then opened and the tank pressure regulator valve set until hose pressure indicates the correct working pressure for the metal to be brazed. Then the torch valve

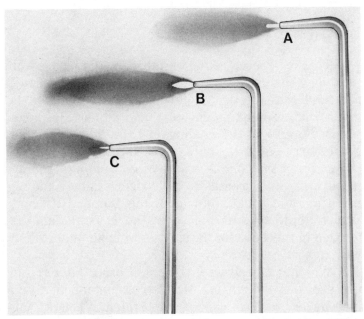

Fig. 7-1. Three brazing flame types. The neutral flame (A) contains an inner cone as shown. Adding more acetylene to the neutral flame creates a carburizing flame (B). A flame heavy in oxygen content creates an oxidizing flame (C).

is closed. The same procedure is followed to set the oxygen hose pressure. With the pressures set, again open the acetylene torch valve and light the acetylene with a friction (spark) lighter. (*Safety note*: Always keep the torch tip facing *away* from the body when igniting or while working.) A sooty yellow flame should emanate. Make sure there is no gap between the flame and torch tip. (A "floating" flame can be blown out with the subsequent introduction of oxygen.) Next, open the torch oxygen valve (very slowly), watching to see that the flame changes to a bluish tinge. The flame should then be adjusted to a neutral, carburizing, or oxidizing flame depending on the heat desired. A neutral flame is the one desired for simple brazing (Fig. 7-1).

Four factors are critical in achieving good welding technique:

- Flame adjustment.
- Flame-to-metal distance.
- Tip angle.
- Welding speed (torch travel).

Thicker metal requires more heat and slower welding speed. Different tip sizes also govern heat, gas, and speed ratios. Follow the recommendations given with the equipment used and adjust the flame to coordinate with the welding job to be done. A neutral flame burns equal amounts of gas and oxygen, leaving the metal chemically the same after welding. Adding more acetylene creates a carburizing flame; adding more oxygen creates an oxidizing flame. Different flames apply to different jobs; the neutral flame is utilized in this book for basic brass brazing undertaken with lighter metals.

Welding a bead with the aid of brass filler rod is not difficult, though practice is recommended if you have never brazed or welded with a torch. When brazing or joining metal with brass filler rod, the torch tip is angled in the direction of travel and the brass rod points in a direction opposite the torch. In welding a bead,

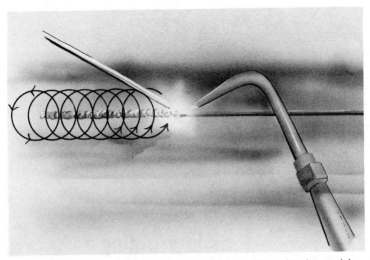

Fig. 7-2. Welding a bead using brass rod. Follow circular and in-and-out movements as described in the text.

the flame is concentrated on the juncture of the two bases to be brazed and a "puddle" (of melted brass) is created, overlapping the joint. At the same time, the rod is pre-heated in the outer envelope of the flame. Then the inner flame cone is brought closer to the rod as the rod is lowered and continuous consecutive motions of this type serve to build the bead. The trick is to lower and raise the rod from the center of the melted puddle. As the rod is withdrawn slightly, it is kept heated by the outer flame. The molten rod, however, must never be allowed to drop into the puddle. The key is to have the rod melted by the melted puddle and flame at the same time, using circular motions as shown in Fig. 7-2.

Plastic Welding

Plastic welding (Fig. 8-1) is a relatively new facet of auto body repair that has emerged because of the ridiculous and exorbitant pricing of new factory replacement parts. Most plastics found on today's autos can be refurbished using this method.

A leading company and pioneer in the plastics welding field is Seelye Inc. of Minneapolis, Minnesota. They market a system that has evolved into the plastic welding standard for most body shops today.

You may be able to find this type of welding equipment on a rental basis. Many of the better and larger equipment rental establishments are providing this tooling since it can be utilized in situations other than automotive.

Two types of plastics are universally utilized in today's automobiles: *thermoplastics* and *thermosets*.

Thermoset plastics undergo a chemical change or "setting" process with the introduction of a catalyzing agent that is mixed into the base material (resin), formulating a new product by the chemical reaction that takes place. A perfect example of a thermoset medium used frequently in automobiles is fiberglass.

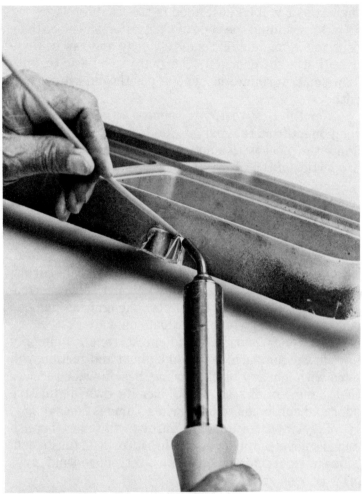

Fig. 8-1. Welding an ABS plastic grille's bolt lug. The round tip is used here since it is more applicable in tight corners (courtesy Seelye Inc.).

Thermosets cannot be welded; their treatment and repair is touched upon elsewhere in this book.

PLASTIC ANALYSIS

Polypropylene, polyurethane, polyethelyne, polyvinyl-chloride, and the frequently utilized ABS are thermoplastic mediums. These materials are weldable and their repair will be described in this chapter.

Determining the type of plastic that the piece to be repaired is made of is relatively easy and can be done by either sight or smell. There are two basic tests to help you determine the type of plastic you are dealing with.

For the first test, you remove a tiny piece of the component from the rear or a hidden portion of the unit, ignite the piece with a match, and observe the burning properties of the plastic.

Polypropylene burns with little physically discernible smoke. It has its own distinctive smell and continues to burn when the flame is removed. It also floats on water.

Polyethylene gives off a waxy odor when ignited. Throughout burning, this material swells, melts, drips, and the drippings also continue burning. This thermoplastic will continue to burn after the igniting flame is removed. Polyethylene also floats on water.

ABS (acrylonitrile butadiene styrene), commonly used in vacuum forming aided by heat and suction, will burn with a heavy black, curling, residue-laden smoke that hangs in the air. ABS has its own distinctive odor and continues to burn when flame is removed.

Polyvinylchloride when burned will self-extinguish upon removal of the flame and has its own distinct smell. This material chars when flame is introduced and gives off a grayish smoke.

Polyurethane is the most flexible of the thermoplastics; it burns with a yellow-orange flame, giving off black smoke. When the flame is removed this material will continue to burn with a sputtering flame.

The second test will help determine what type of plastic welding rod is compatible with the component to be welded.

First, melt a sample piece of the material you are to repair along with the plastic welding rod you think is appropriate for the situation involved. Then melt a piece of the selected rod. While the two are still in a warm or melted state, contact the melted locations briefly, then try to pull them apart. If the two materials are unfusable, then they are incompatible and differ in thermoplastic structure.

The procedure for welding plastic is similar to that of welding metal but more simplified. Practice is advised but the proper knack can be achieved in a short time.

PLASTIC WELDING TECHNIQUE

Tack Welding is the preliminary step in the welding procedure. A special tacking tip is supplied with each welding outfit and this tip is utilized for spot-tacking pieces to be joined, particularly if the crack is long or the damage extensive. Cracks in the plastic should be tacked the entire length by drawing the point of the tack welding tip along the torn pieces as they are aligned in place. The hot tip should be applied firmly and *evenly* on both sides of the crack. In obtrusive areas, cracks and tears should be tacked and even welded from behind or underneath.

Round tip welding is applicable where cracks or damage may be in hard-to-reach areas or where confined sharp corners exist. The round tip is also widely utilized for filling small holes. In this procedure, the proper compatible plastic weld-rod material is selected and the end cut to a 60 degree angle with knife or cutters. The plastic rod is then placed at a right angle to the crack where the damage starts. The iron tip is applied to the rod until it melts and becomes tacky. Then the rod is forced into the joint firmly, using the hot tip for melting and fusing along the length of the crack. The tip of the rod should point away from the direction of the weld. (Study the procedure in Figs. 8-2 through 8-9.) A solid bond is important at the start of the weld. After the rod is initially secured, recommence heating the weld joint and rod together, implementing a slight fanning motion, then continue in line along the crack with the proceeding weld beading. Exert firm downward pressure along the weld joint as the material is fused. If

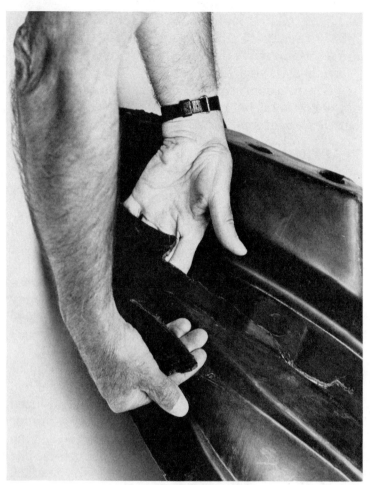

Fig. 8-2. In this sequence we know typical repair procedure for this damaged front fender skirt. The material is polypropylene.

the weld is properly executed, a small, neat bead will form along both edges of the weld while a small roll forms ahead of the welded rod. To finish off the weld, the rod is held down and cut, and the end heat-formed neatly into the surface of the repaired piece.

High-speed welding is ideally suited to auto body-work use and is applied with a third type of tip known as a *high-speed tip*. With this repair system, the plastic welding rod is again cut at a 60 degree angle, but this time inserted into a specially designed feeder tube that is an integral part of the high-speed tip. The rod tack and welding commences as in the prior procedures. At the onset, the rod is manually fed into the feeder tube, the rod again situated at a 90 degree angle to the surface to start the weld. The softened end of the rod is pressed into the joint with the curved foot of the high-speed tip. The tip is then repositioned to a 45 degree angle and the welder moved along the joint. After the weld bead is started, manual rod feeding is unnecessary as the rod will feed through the tube automatically.

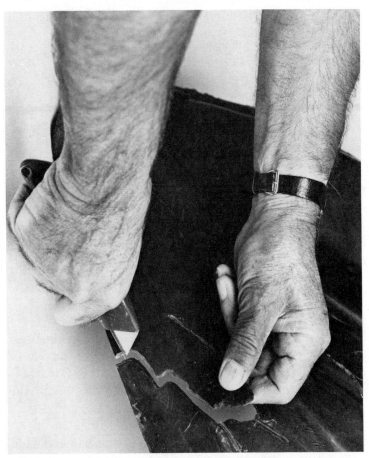

Fig. 8-3. Torn edges are beveled in order to channel a groove in preparation for tacking.

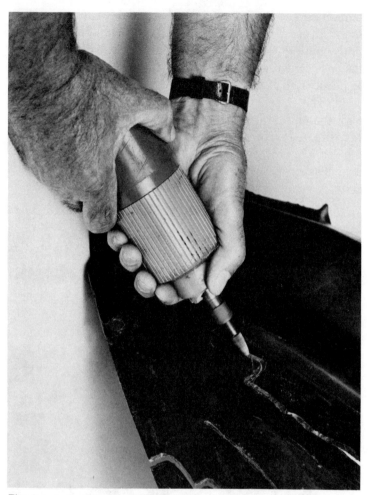
Fig. 8-4. A die grinder may also be used to channel a groove.

Some precautions should be taken with high-speed plastic welding in order to ensure fault-free fusion of cracks and joints. Once the welding procedure is started, the tip must be kept in continuous motion along the joint since the tip is constantly melting the rod.

Study the weld bead forming and adjust the speed and heat accordingly. To terminate the high-speed weld (if the rod is not fully used), the rod is "set" with firm pressure and the tip pulled off the weld. The weld end may be trimmed with a knife. Remove the remaining rod piece from the feeder tube immediately or it will continue to melt, clogging the tube. The feeder foot should be cleaned often with a wire brush.

A good firm weld, whether done with the round or high-speed tip, will not pull apart and in many instances will be stronger than areas adjacent to the weld bead.

To achieve a quality weld, ensure the following:

■ The welding rod must be manipulated so that it

Fig. 8-5. Edges are pulled apart and a hand grinder applied to ensure a proper tacking channel.

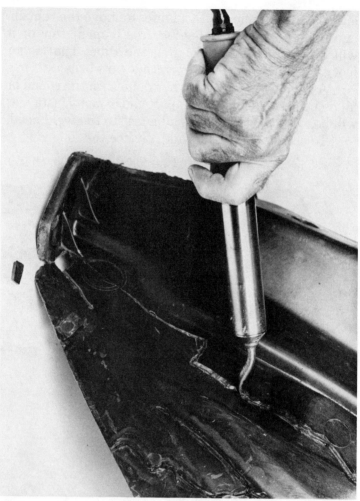

Fig. 8-6. The tacking tip is used to achieve a hinge bond between edges. Clamping together prior to tacking may also be necessary.

holds its round shape; utilize proper rod movement and welding tip temperatures.
- Check to see that a proper bead forms along each side of the weld and positive fusion is realized.
- Make sure rod material or base material does not char or change color.

- Don't stretch the rod over the weld; rod length used should match joint or crack length.
- Follow instructions provided explicitly; never use oxygen or flammable gases with the welder, only air.

A typical plastic welding procedure is shown in Figs. 8-1 through 8-8 using the Seelye welding system.

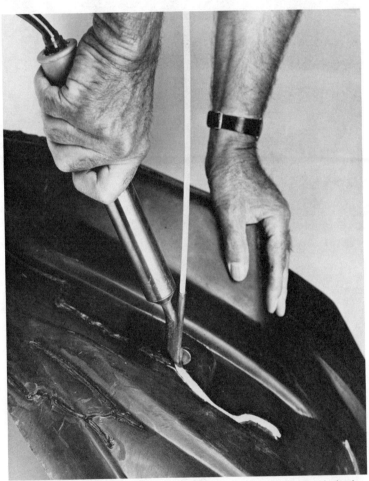

Fig. 8-7. High-speed welding using the high-speed tip for a relatively long crack. White polypropylene welding rod is used here only for photo clarity.

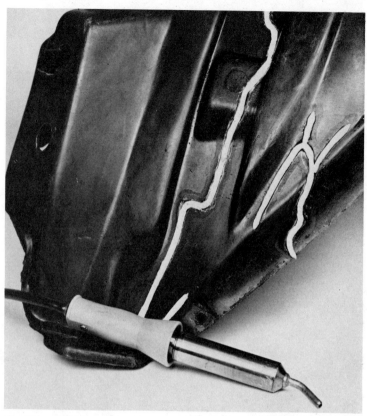

Fig. 8-8. Here the round tip was used since the cracks were short and contained tight turns.

Table 8-1.
Thermoplastic Welding Temperature Guide (courtesy Seelye Inc.).

	Polyvinyl chloride	Poly-ethylene	Poly-propylene	ABS	Poly-urethane
Welding Rod Color Code	Light Grey	Brown	Black	Blue	Clear
Welding Temperature	525	550	575	500	500
Forming Temperature	300	300	350	300	300
Welding Gas	Air	Air*	Air*	Air	Air
Recommended Pressure	3	3	3	3	4

All temperatures shown are degrees Fahrenheit.

*Nitrogen gas optional

(All photos and procedures courtesy of Seelye Inc.)

Table 8-1 will guide you toward proper plastic welding technique.

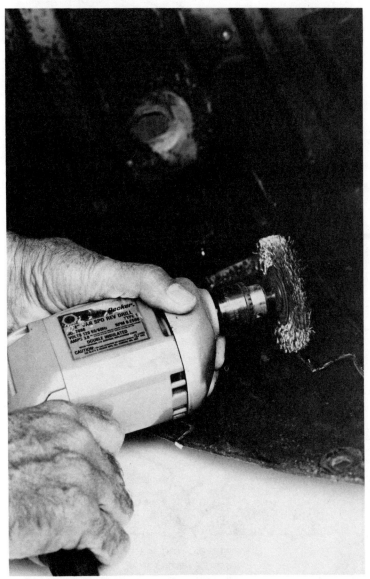

Fig 8-9. Back side of welded fender skirt showing how a power brush serves to remove excess and cosmetically clean area. Excess may also be removed and finished off with sandpaper.

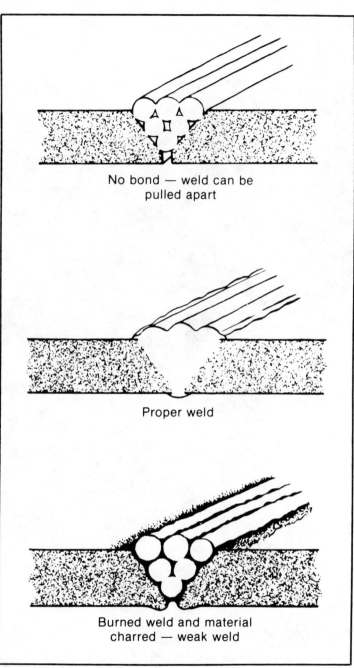

No bond — weld can be
pulled apart

Proper weld

Burned weld and material
charred — weak weld

Fig. 8-10. Welding analysis . (courtesy Seelye Inc.)

Windows, Doors,
Trunk Lids, and Hoods

Many accident cases involve doors, windows, trunks, and hoods. Their repair, replacement, and adjustment will be covered in this chapter. Much of the work is within the realm of the Saturday mechanic.

WINDOWS

Automobile glass can be broken down into two broad categories: *door windows* and *windshields*. Windshields (along with rear windows) are relatively simple to replace; door windows can pose a problem, unless they are of the fixed type (which is rare).

In replacing an operating window, there are related integrated mechanisms involved; some may be quite complex (Fig. 9-1). The mechanisms include a *run channel*, *cranks* (or electric motors), and *lift bars*; all must be properly aligned in order for the window to operate properly without binding. To obtain access to door mechanisms, interior door paneling must also be removed. This procedure can also be quite complex.

If you are not super handy or familiar with the mechanical end of door window replacement, you are better off taking the job to window replacement spe-

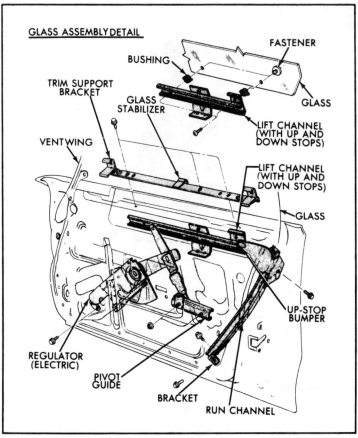

Fig. 9-1. A typical door window operating mechanism. (courtesy Chrysler Corp.)

cialists. In most instances, they will insert the window they sell you at an added cost that is not too prohibitive. If you intend to tackle the job yourself, make sure beforehand that you have a shop manual for your car on hand in order to simplify the exchange procedure involved.

WINDSHIELDS AND REAR WINDOWS

Windshields and rear windows are easy for the do-it-yourselfer. The hardest part of the entire operation is the removal of the old windshield, since safety precautions must be taken — especially if the glass is firmly set in the window flange.

Windshields are secured (and waterproofed) with a butyl seal that runs around the perimeter of the windshield flange and a locking strip (usually a chrome molding) that snaps on around the edge of the windshield. The moldings are held on by clips spaced at intervals around the windshield; these are retained by pins. Clips are snapped onto the pins and the moldings snapped onto the clips (after the glass is in place). The clips are placed prior to the insertion of the windshield. In most cases, when you remove an old windshield, the old clips will be reusable. If damaged, they can be snapped out and new replacements snapped in. This procedure also applies to rear windows.

In windshield replacement, removal of the old or damaged glass is the most tedious part of the operation. In replacement of windshields and rear windows, an extra pair of hands is strongly advised so as not to damage the glass, which is large and hard to maneuver.

Before the glass can be removed, the moldings (locking strips) must come off. This operation is facilitated by using the Lisle 6470 locking strip tool; it is specifically designed for removing moldings and locking strips. Lisle also markets a handy windshield remover tool. These tools are shown in Fig. 9-2. Before removing the windshield, remove the windshield wipers.

To remove the glass, which is sealed with a butyl strip, you must first break the seal. This is done using a two-foot piece of steel wire secured to a handle at each end (Fig. 9-3). One end of the wire is squeezed through the seal and pulled into the interior of the car, where a wooden handle (1 inch dowel) is secured. The seal is then broken by cutting with the wire, using a sawing motion all around the perimeter of the glass. This process involves two people, one inside and one outside the car. After the glass is removed, be sure to remove

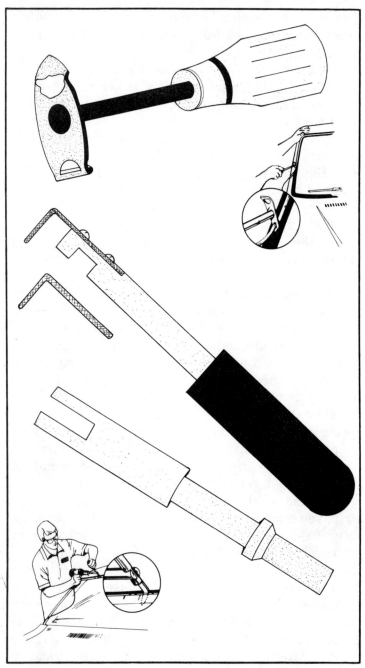

Fig. 9-2. Two special tools by Lisle aid greatly in windshield removal.

Fig. 9-3. Cutting butyl seals in order to remove windshield glass.
(courtesy Chrysler Corp.).

all traces of the butyl tape with a knife and solvent
(wax and grease remover).

Replacing the windshield is not difficult. First coat
the windshield (or rear window) flange with Window-
Weld sealer, a solution that is applied by brush. Then
Window Weld Butyl sealer (in a strip form) is applied
around the circumference of the flange about a half inch
from the inner edge. The sealer affixes itself and is

Fig. 9-4. Molding retainer clips. Located around the window flange,
they serve to hold snap-on moldings.

Fig. 9-5. After the butyl sealer is affixed, the windshield is placed in position and pressed into the sealer strip around the edges.

further retained by the sealer applied previously. Check to see that all the molding clips are in place and in good condition (Fig. 9-4).

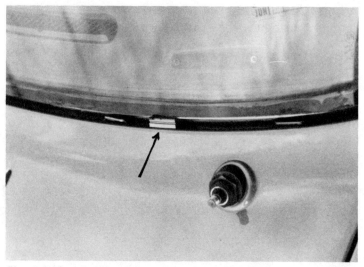

Fig. 9-6. Small pillow blocks serve in windshield alignment and placement.

Fig. 9-7. Snapping on the chrome molding strips finishes the job.

Next the windshield is positioned and the edges pressed down firmly against the butyl stripping (Fig. 9-5). For proper alignment, the glass must rest on the small pillow blocks located in the lower windshield flange area (Fig. 9-6). These alignment and support blocks are found in this general area in all cars. Some have one; some have two. They're either on the sides of the lower edges or in the center.

Firmly press the glass onto the butyl sealant by going all around the perimeter of the glass and checking that glass and strip are in positive contact. When the glass is positively secured, the moldings are snapped into place (Fig. 9-7). If this procedure is closely followed and no gaps are left in the butyl sealer strip, the windshield will be firmly fixed and fully waterproof.

PAINTED MOLDINGS

A number of today's vehicles sport flat black-painted moldings instead of chrome ones. These painted moldings tend to flake or wear away with time and exposure to the elements, affecting the car's overall

Fig. 9-8. Typical wear is exhibited on this painted Corvette window molding.

Fig. 9-9. The molding strips are masked off and newspaper is added around the edges to inhibit overspray.

appearance. This problem can easily and quickly be remedied.

Figure 9-8 shows the molding strip on a Corvette with the overcoating worn thin. First the metal strip to be painted is masked all around with ¾'' masking tape, then the outer edges are masked with newspaper to control overspray (Fig. 9-9). All the molding to be painted is sanded with 400 grit sandpaper; then the metal is wiped clean with a rag slightly dampened in Prepsol or similar wax and grease remover medium and spray painted with flat black aerosol paint readily available at auto supply shops (Fig. 9-10). Keep the can about a foot away when spraying and use quick side-to-side motions, building up the color in stages. Allow each previous application to fully dry before the next coat is applied. Figure 9-11 shows the finished refurbished molding.

DOORS

Damaged doors can be repaired with plastic filler if the damage is minor and confined to dents and dings;

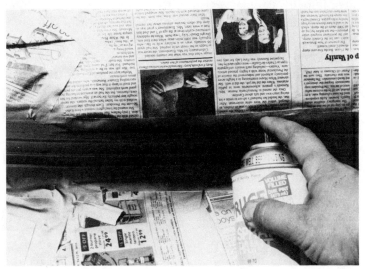

Fig. 9-10. The moldings are sprayed (see text).

Fig. 9-11. The finished job exhibits a "like new" appearance.

the door may have to be replaced if damage is radical and affects alignment and operation. If the outer surface of the door is badly dented or torn, and the internal window mechanism is intact, you can easily solve the problem by replacing the outer surface with a "door skin" replacement available at auto dealers. The skin replaces the original piece, which is usually attached by edge crimping and tack welding.

If the door is destroyed, replacing the entire door is the only route to take. You can buy a new door or use a salvage yard replacement. The latter is the best possible solution. It will be cheaper and involve nothing more than repainting and replacement. Just be sure that the replacement door is in sound working condition and in good shape externally. Replacement involves removing the hinge bolts and bolting in and aligning the new door.

DOOR ALIGNMENT

Door misalignment is frequently caused by simple

bump accidents or wear and age. A few simple alignment tricks are presented here that anyone can use
with positive results.

Figure 9-12 shows a typical misaligned door. The
door drops in the rear and does not close in proper
alignment. It also kinks toward the front (Fig. 9-13).
An easy solution is simple and primitive but effective.
A 2×4 is inserted in the door sill under the door and
pressure is exerted upward using the 2×4 as a lever.
This is done by adding pressure in increments until
the door comes into alignment. This method is particularly effective if a bent hinge is the cause of the misalignment.

Another solution is the use of washers or shims
behind the hinges (see Fig. 9-14) to control a high or
low misaligned door. Another method to raise a door is
shown in Fig. 9-15; a jack is used working against the
weight of the car to straighten the hinges. When the
door spacing is even and unbinding, the door is in
proper alignment.

Fig. 9-12. A common door alignment problem: the door sags toward
the rear.

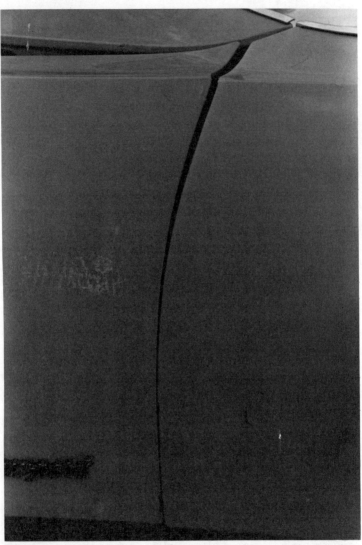

Fig. 9-13. The sagging door kinks toward the front, causing binding and paint chipping in the adjacent frame.

HOODS AND DECK LIDS (TRUNKS)

Hoods and trunk lids must frequently be replaced due to accident damage. In cases where minor dents and dings prevail, body filler will solve the problem — save for edge kinks, which will inhibit proper alignment and sealing. In severe cases it is more feasible to replace rather than fix a damaged hood as they can be obtained from auto salvage sources at prices far below that of a new hood or trunk.

Removal of hood and deck lids is a two-man operation due to the bulk and weight involved. Removal of

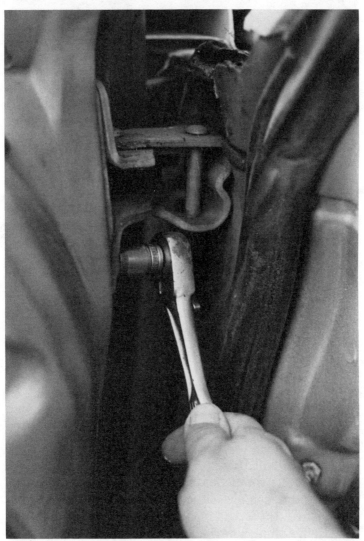

Fig. 9-14. Washers and shims placed behind hinges will help alleviate alignment problems in some instances.

Fig. 9-15. Realigning a door with a scissors jack.

hinge bolts will free the hood or deck while in open positions; the components can then be lifted off. Some hoods and decks also involve torsion bars or springs. If attached, these will also have to be unfastened.

Reinstalling a new hood also requires another person's assistance. One person maintains the hood (or trunk) in position while the second inserts the hinge retainers.

Salvage replacement hoods or trunk lids will have old hinge alignment marks in the proper places; when positioning the replacement component, use them as guides. Minor alignment adjustments will most likely be needed, as not all hoods and lids align exactly. Elongated holes in the hinges allow for deviations in lateral and back-and-forth positioning. The cowl-to-hood adjustment should be made first, then the side spacing adjustments. Latches and catches can also be moved somewhat to aid in proper alignment. Latches can be shifted laterally and strikers can be adjusted up or down. In some cases, hinges may need straightening; this can be done by exerting heavy force or as in the case of doors, using a 2×4.

Front Body Panel
and Component Repair

Repair and replacement of areas forward of the windshield post is relatively simple (with the exclusion of engine damage) for the layman. Repair of simple dings, dents and header panel, hood, and windshield damage has already been covered in other portions of this book. This chapter will cover the remaining areas.

FRONT FENDERS

Front fenders are easily replaced if a body repair job is too difficult for the do-it-yourselfer to undertake. Ninety-eight percent of the front fenders on all cars today are bolt-on units involving only R&R (a professional term meaning *removal and replacement*). For the neophyte, R&R can be both easy and cheaper in the long run — particularly in front fender work, a bolt-on operation involving common tools that are less specialized than equipment needed for other types of bodywork. Fenders can be removed easily, quickly, and with little fuss using socket wrenches, box wrenches, or even basic adjustable wrenches (Fig. 10-1).

The typical fender attaches to the inner motor compartment panels at the top about an inch or so

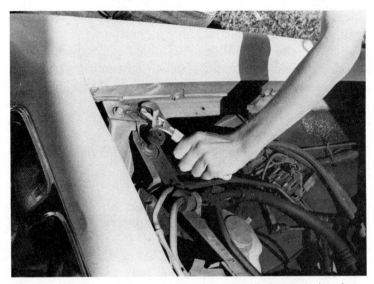

Fig. 10-1. Virtually all fender components are bolt-secured and remove easily.

from the hood line. Access to these securing bolts is usually unobstructed, making removal even simpler. Fenders usually have bolt holes or retaining tabs to conform to the motor compartment securing points, and also at the bottoms of the fender sections where they attach to adjacent sheet metal body parts or securing struts.

The fender removal process is very basic. The only drawbacks to be encountered involve the bolts that secure the fender component in place. If these are rusted in place, the rust will have to be broken loose. Apply penetrating oil or tap a stubborn bolt with a hammer if it refuses to break loose by hand. If the bolt still remains immobile, then go into the hammer-and-chisel routine. A sharp hammer-and-chisel blow to a stubborn bolt will often allow the securing nut to expand enough to turn when torque is subsequently applied. If all else fails, revert to the old standby of cutting with a hacksaw; in the long run this will necessitate a new bolt and nut in reassembly. Prior to tackling fender removal, take off all lights, attached grille component pieces, and connective wiring.

After the top fender bolts have been broken loose, leave them in place and proceed to remove *first* the single bottom securing bolts found on most fenders; these screw into the cowl panel or a securing strut. Then remove the cowl side panel bolts found at the rear and accessible only when the door is opened. Then remove the valance panel and grille panel bolts. Remove all wheel well bolts. At this point the fender will be held in place by the loosened top engine compartment bolts. (Also at this point some model cars may require a bumper removal before the fender can come off. If necessary remove the bumper; this is again a straight-forward bolt-removal operation.)

Now the loosened top fender bolts can be removed, disengaging the fender completely. If these top bolts are not removed *last*, the fender could jostle loose and shift, hindering lower bolt removal; the fender could also fall on the person removing it as he removes a final lower bolt.

In securing the new panel, the top bolts are put in *first* (loosely), then the lower ones. When the fender is jockeyed into proper alignment, all the bolts can be firmly torqued down.

HEADER PANELS

Header panels are the cowl pieces that usually hold the headlights and grilles. These were at one time all steel. Some are still of steel (or zinc or aluminum castings) but due to cost, the auto manufacturers are starting to use fiberglass and exotic plastic molded units. In many cases they can be repaired and patched (see fiberglass repair chapter). The R&R approach is also practical with header panels as it involves only simple bolt removal. In virtually all cases, grilles and headlights must be removed to allow access to some of the header panel attachment bolts. When replacing header panels, use care in torquing down the bolts —

torquing them too tightly may cause the fiberglass to crack around the bolt holes.

GRILLES

Removing and replacing grilles is child's play. They usually come off with the removal of four or more bolts and in many cases are secured with screws (Fig. 10-2). Most grilles today are made of plastic or cast metal. Many of the molded types are held on by speed nuts and molded-in bolts accessible only from the rear. Screw-on grilles are usually accessible from the front and can be replaced with a Phillips screwdriver.

Some grilles contain a spring-loaded mounting setup that allows the grille to traverse back under moderate impact. This type can jam in its rearward position and may have to be realigned and adjusted as part of the repair or replacement procedure.

Grilles vary widely in type and mounting. Study each individual case carefully before beginning repair or removal.

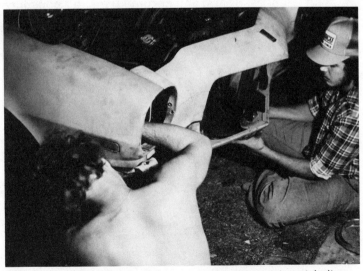

Fig. 10-2. Grilles, headlights, etc., are for the most part bolt on-installations--easily removed and accessible.

Fig. 10-3. Headlight bezels and trim can be removed with a simple screwdriver.

HEADLIGHTS

Headlights and headlight bezels, directional lights, and marker lights all fall into the minor repair category. Damaged lenses, lights, and chrome trim and housings should be replaced rather than repaired. These tasks are easily undertaken with only a screwdriver (Fig. 10-3).

Interior Components and Cosmetics

A major portion of interior rejuvenation and restoration consists of cleaning with special solvents and repairing and repainting plastic interior modular parts.

There are basically three types of fabrics utilized in car interiors: synthetics (rayon, nylon), leather, and leather imitations (vinyl, Mylar, Naugahyde, etc.). Leather is rarely used except in luxury cars.

Synthetic cloth-like materials can be cleaned with basic detergents if soiling and staining is minor, or with highly volatile cleaners for heavy stains and discoloration. The volatile cleaners are generally applied to break down grease, oil, oil-based paint, etc. Be sure to read and follow instructions carefully if you use volatile cleaners; use one *specifically* formulated for the *particular* fabric you will be cleaning. Use of the wrong "hot" cleaner will damage or melt the fabric surface or attack the color finish.

USING SOLVENTS

When using solvents, allow the *chemical* action to do the cleaning work. Never rub too vigorously or too hard in its application. Use a clean, soft cloth (baby diaper material is great), dampening it with the applicable solvent.

With a slight circular motion and moderate pressure, rub all over the soiled area. With larger stains, work from the outer edge of the stain towards its center and repeat until the soiled area is fully cleaned. Change to a clean spot on the cloth after *each* rubout procedure; using the same section of cloth twice will only serve to spread and reapply some of the dirt.

When the area is clean, pick up excess solvent in the fabric by pressing a blotter against it to soak up excess moisture. Allow the cleaner to dry completely. It is better to apply cleaners conservatively to avoid oversaturation. Remember, some cleaners can affect some upholstery materials, especially foam rubber. Stubborn stains may require repeated applications of cleaner to break down the soiling medium.

Keep in mind that most volatile cleaners are toxic and flammable. Use rubber gloves, work in adequately ventilated areas (preferably outdoors), avoid inhalation of the vapors, and don't smoke or allow any open flame or ignition source in your work area.

Detergents work quite well with synthetic fabrics. Apply a strong solution of detergent and warm water to the fabric surface and use moderate pressure to rub out the stain or soilage; use a second clean dampened cloth to remove excess detergent and dirt. A final rubout with a clean dry cloth completes the procedure if all discoloration is removed on initial cleaning. Repeated applications of detergent may be required if all soilage is not removed the first time.

Refrain from using detergents or cleaning solutions containing water on cottons and broadcloths as they mar the finish of the cloth.

Leather is best cleaned with saddle soap, followed by application of a good leather dressing.

Vinyls, Naugahydes, and similar coated fabrics should not be cleaned with volatile solvents. Use damp cloths or mild or general-purpose detergents. Vinyl cleaners or dressings (Armorall is one popular brand) are also excellent cleaners and preservatives for coated fabrics.

Carpets in automobiles are similar to carpets in the home, and should be treated in the same fashion. Carpets should first be brushed and vacuumed. If badly soiled or stained, they can successfully be cleaned with rug shampoo. Some volatile cleaners can be applied to carpets but should be administered sparingly as they can remove some of the coloring.

TREATING TYPICAL UPHOLSTERY STAINS

Candy, Syrup: Rub damaged area with hot water-soaked cloth. Neutral soap will also work in a warm wet cloth. If stain persists, try a volatile cleaner.

Gum: After chewing gum has hardened, pull it away and scrape away remaining sticky residue. If reside remains, break it down with a volatile cleaner and scrape it away with a dull edged blade while soft.

Fruit and Liquor: Best removed with very hot water or light application of a volatile cleaner.

Chocolate and Ice Cream: Rub area first with cloth dipped in hot water. When dry, apply a volatile cleaner and blot the area until cleaner and stain is removed.

Oil and Grease: Volatile cleaners work best here as heavy oils and greases are somewhat impervious to detergents and water.

PLASTIC INTERIOR COMPONENTS

Occasionally interior plastic parts (dash, instrument consoles, door panels) become damaged or discolored. These component parts are relatively simple to repair and repaint if not severely damaged.

Figure 11-1 shows an inside front plastic door panel of the type commonly found in many of today's cars. This plastic part (seen from behind) shows a crack

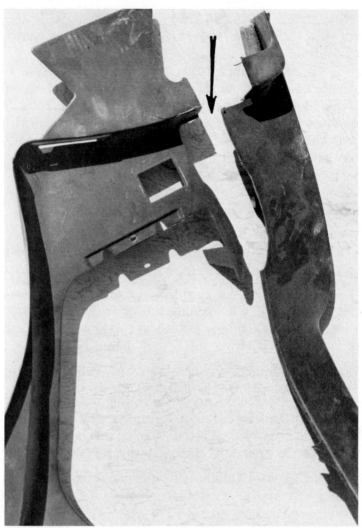

Fig. 11-1. Typical cracked inner door panel (plastic).

separating the top and bottom portions (arrow). The piece will have to be joined, reinforced from the rear, the crack filled in from the front, and finally repainted.

First the area to be rejoined is sanded with 80-grit sandpaper on its back side. The best medium for joining these interior plastic components is a two-part automotive epoxy. (A recommended brand is Resco, available

Fig. 11-2. Disjointed pieces are tacked.

at body and hardware suppliers.) The two-part adhesive is mixed thoroughly and applied to the edges of the cracks. The two disjointed parts are brought together, then set aside and allowed to dry till they are securely tacked (Fig. 11-2). Fiberglass cloth or vinyl screening

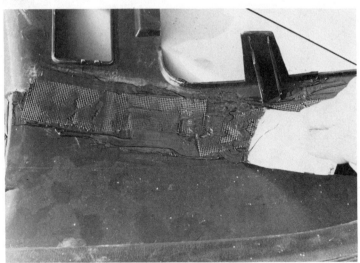

Fig. 11-3. Rear is reinforced with fiberglass cloth or mesh.

Fig. 11-4. Crack on front side is filled in.

is then placed over the crack and additional epoxy is squeegeed on as shown in Fig. 11-3. When fully cured and hardened (usually a matter of eight hours), the panel is turned around to the grained interior facade

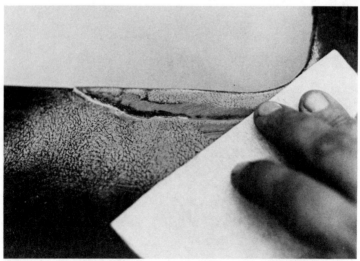
Fig. 11-5. When dried, repair area is sanded smooth and repainted. If properly finished, the repair will be unnoticeable.

and the crack remaining at the joint is filled in (Fig. 11-4). Excess epoxy is removed. When this "filler" application is fully dried it is sanded smooth until the joint is undiscernable (Fig. 11-5). The panel can then be repainted with the proper color lacquer recommended on the car's color code sticker.

Vinyl Tops

Vinyl top replacement is a job for the pros and should not be tackled by the novice. It involves gluing, stretching, heat forming, and sophisticated trimming and joining that is best left to the experts. However, a vinyl top that is still in good shape can be saved or refurbished to look as good as new.

TEARS AND GOUGES

Tears, gouges, and cuts in vinyl tops are not easy to repair because the vinyl was stretched when it was put on and shrinks as it is exposed to the sun. Minor repairs by the do-it-yourselfer can equal those done by professional patchers, but at best the condition can only be improved, not totally eliminated. The only way to obtain perfect results is to get a new top installed professionally.

To repair a small tear, first clean the overall damaged area with vinyl cleaner or conditioner in order to soften it. Softening the vinyl will make it easier for you to stretch the torn portion so that the edges will meet when tacked. Next, coat the underside of the torn flap and outer edges with vinyl glue, which can be obtained from auto shop suppliers in aerosol cans or squeeze bottles. Stretch the edges and move them together as you press the torn portion into place. Clean off any excess glue. If done correctly, the repair won't be too noticeable.

New vinyl pastes are also available; they are used in conjunction with vinyl grain-forming irons that melt and fuse the paste and adjacent areas so that the repair is almost undiscernable. These heat patch repair kits may also be found in auto body shop suppliers.

REPAINTING AND DYEING

The most successful approach to rejuvenating vinyl tops is repainting and dyeing. Special vinyl dyes are marketed that match all OEM factory colors. They can be sprayed on with a production auto spray gun.

Standard acrylic lacquers can also be used for spraying vinyl tops and are frequently used in all body shops. Before painting with acrylics, a flex agent must be added to the acrylic lacquer in proportions specified by the manufacturer. This flex agent gives the acrylic paint extra elasticity so that it will not crack

Fig. 12-1. Top is masked using tape and paper.

Fig. 12-2. Top is sprayed. Three to four coats should suffice in order to impart a new look to the top.

when exposed to natural shrinkage, sunlight, or temperature changes. The flex agent also helps promote better adhesion to the vinyl due to the elasticity it imparts to the lacquer.

Whether you choose to use vinyl dye or acrylic

Fig. 12-3. The repainted vinyl top.

lacquer with a flex agent additive, the application procedure is the same. First, all the vinyl should be wiped clean and prepped with wax and grease remover, then wash away or wipe off all solvents prior to painting. Any necessary patching or repair to the vinyl should be executed now if necessary. Mask off all chrome, windows, and body areas adjacent to the vinyl top as shown in Fig. 12-1. Then spray on the vinyl dye or acrylic lacquer with flex agent additive (Fig. 12-2). The final results can be seen in Fig. 12-3.

Bumpers

Bumpers cause perhaps the fewest problems in body repair, though not necessarily the least expensive — especially if a new one is called for.

METAL BUMPERS

Damaged steel-and-chrome bumpers can rarely be repaired or returned to their original state without reshaping, welding, and rechroming; in virtually all cases this is even costlier than a new unit. The best solution is to replace the unit with a new or used bumper. The most reasonable alternative is replacement with a used bumper. Used bumpers can be economically obtained from salvage yards and will vary in condition from excellent to disgusting. "Shopping around" through several salvage yards — though a bit time-consuming — will eventually result in finding a satisfactory replacement.

Replacing a bumper is a simple undertaking; most are secured by four strong bolts that can be removed with simple tools such as box, ratchet, or adjustable monkey wrenches.

Some steel bumpers will exhibit only minor damage

such as scratches and gouges in the chrome plating. These scratches in the chrome film can lead to the steel underneath eventually rusting. Touching up with aluminum paint will inhibit the rusting, but the results are not very attractive — and often the rust can work its way through the paint.

An old body shop trick that works is retouching the scratches or gouges with solder. The procedure is simple: first, all the rust in the scratches is cleaned or scraped out with a knife or needle file. Then Duzall or a similar flux is applied to clean the scratches and break down the remaining oxides. Heat is then applied with a soldering iron to the scratch until the flux bubbles or flows. Then the area is touched with solder wire, allowing the wire to melt and flow into the scratch. The flux is washed away and the area cleaned with a cloth saturated with wax and grease solvent. The area is final-finished by buffing to a bright finish; the polished solder should match up well to the adjacent chrome and should retain its brightness. Most important, the solder will cover and seal the exposed metal, guarding against further oxidation and corrosion.

RUBBER BUMPERS

The hot setup on modern vehicles (particularly some of the imports) is the rubber bumper or rubber bumper wraparound, in which a plastic-rubber sleeve is utilized over a metal undersupport. The rubber overpiece is very susceptible to damage whenever bumper-to-bumper accidents occur. These torn, punctured rubber pieces can be simply and inexpensively repaired. Buying new rubber bumpers is inadvisable — even body shops go the repair route as it is foolproof and far, far cheaper than new replacement.

Practical rubber bumper repair is now possible with the introduction of new miracle adhesive kits that fully repair and fill in damaged areas.

One of the best is the Marson Flex bumper repair

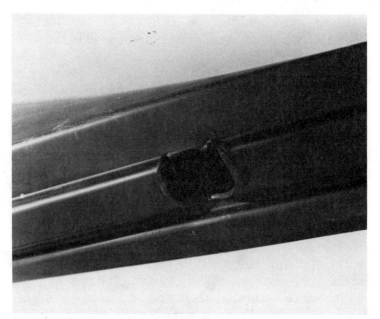

Fig. 13-1. Perforation in bumper cover.

kit, which contains an adhesive filler, reinforcement screening, and applicators. The adhesive filter is a two-part flex resin/catalyst formula that is mixed in equal parts of resin and hardener.

Figure 13-1 shows a typical problem for application of the flex bumper repair procedure. The rubber bumper cover shown has been perforated, leaving an opening of about two inches — a noticeable rupture to say the least. The problem requires patching as well as filling to bridge the gap properly.

Cut a piece from another section of the rubber cover or rubber bumper scrap and glue it to the rear of the opening with the flex resin, overlapping the edges (Fig. 13-2). Allow the patch to fully fuse and adhere to the bumper.

When the patch is firmly secure, mix up another batch of flex filler. Apply this to the front of the bumper, filling in the hole completely (Fig. 13-3). Don't be skimpy; if you overfill it, it can be sanded and trimmed

Fig. 13-2. Back of hole is patched with piece of similar bumper material.

down. After the filler is fully cured (proper drying time will be specified in the instructions), the repaired section can be sanded and contoured with 80-grit sand-

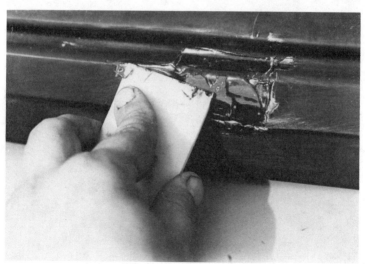

Fig. 13-3. Front is filled in.

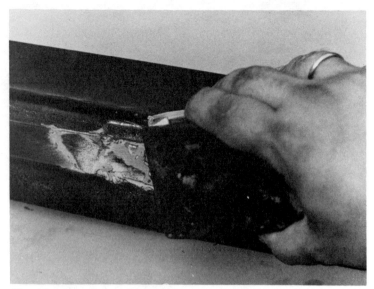

Fig. 13-4. Repair area is sanded and contoured.

paper, followed by final smoothing with 180-grit sand-paper (Fig. 13-4). Figure 13-5 shows the completed repair area smoothed out and ready for paint.

Fig. 13-5. Finished fill-in repair.

Rust Work

Simple rust work not involving metal patching and welding can be undertaken by anyone, as this chapter will show.

There are a number of effective ways to remove rust. The simplest is by grinding. A grinder with a 36-grit disk is applied as shown in Fig. 14-1, grinding through the rust and down to bare metal. Hand-sanding with 36-grit sandpaper will also work, but it is time-consuming and not as effective as machine grinding.

The best method by far involves the use of a sandblaster. A sandblaster can be rented for a few hours, which is all the time you need to complete even the largest rust blasting job.

Figure 14-2 shows a typical rust patch. In Fig. 14-3, a blast of sand is directed onto the rusted area with the tip of the sandblaster nozzle held about four inches away from the rusted surface. The nozzle is moved over the entire area until all the rust is removed (Fig. 14-4).

Figure 14-5 shows a more radical type of corrosion; this should be first sandblasted and then filled in since the metal is corroded all the way through. Once the metal is blasted, it should be treated with a metal prep solution.

Fig. 14-1. Grinding is a simple approach to rust removal.(courtesy Chicago Pneumatic)

Filling in and covering rust holes and badly corroded areas is best accomplished using a metal-impregnated body filler such as Evercoat Pure Metal. The procedure is simple and described step by step in Figs. 14-6 through 14-11, in which a badly rusted area at the rear of a door frame and directly underneath a vinyl top perimeter is patched. First all destroyed metal is

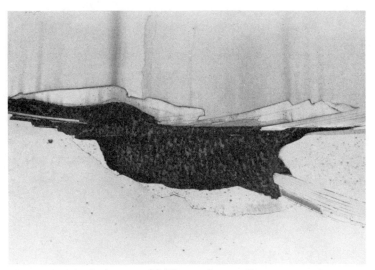

Fig. 14-2. A typical area exhibiting surface rust.

chipped away (Fig. 14-6) and the adjacent areas sand-blasted to remove all rust traces (Fig. 14-7).

Then some fiberglass cloth impregnated with catalyzed Pure Metal is laid over the area to seal all gaps

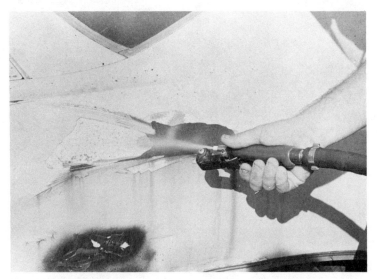

Fig. 14-3. Rust is blasted away by sandblaster. The sandblaster used here is Brut Model 70S pressure blaster, a small but highly efficient unit.

115

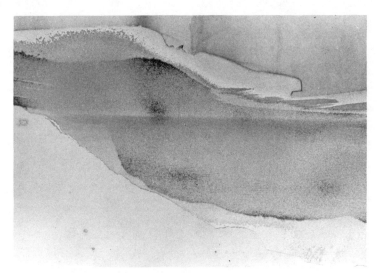

Fig. 14-4. The same area blasted completely free of rust.

produced by the severe corrosion (Fig. 14-8). When the
metal-impregnated cloth patches have hardened (after
a few hours), an overall skim coating of Pure Metal is

Fig. 14-5. Radical rust spots must be blasted, then patched with a
rust-resistant filler.

Fig. 14-6. First all rust is removed.

Fig. 14-7. The metal is reshaped and sandblasted.

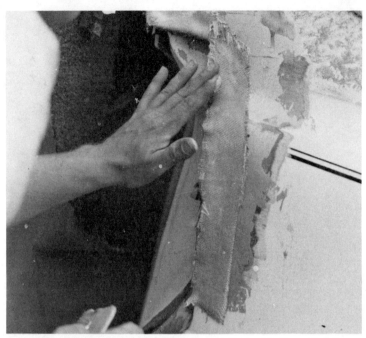

Fig. 14-8. Fiberglass cloth strips impregnated with Pure Metal are used to cover the rusted-out gaps.

Fig. 14-9. A topcoating of Pure Metal is applied after the filler-impregnated cloth strips have hardened.

118

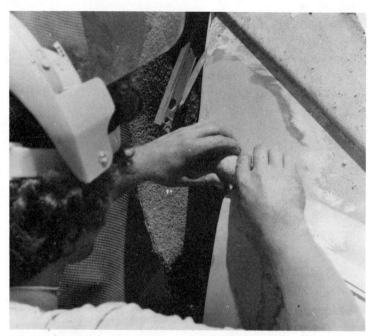

Fig. 14-10. The area is blocked and sanded smooth.

Fig. 14-11. The finished patchwork ready for priming and painting.

squeegeed on (Fig. 14-9). After the light overcoating has hardened it can be sanded down or shaped with 80-grit sandpaper before the skim coat has set but not fully hardened (Fig. 14-10).

Coating and patching with a metal-impregnated filler assures a troublefree, long-lasting rust repair job. The metal filler is rustproof and waterproof, non-porous, and provides excellent adhesion to sandblasted or ground metal. After the filler has been feathered and smoothed out, it can be primed and painted (Fig. 14-11).

Figures 14-2 through 14-11 were provided by Mark Genet of the Import Shop, Pompano Beach, Florida.

Frame and Alignment Work

Frame and alignment corrections are necessary in cases involving heavy collision and radical damage, particularly to frames and front ends of the newer cars with unibody structure.

Unfortunately, corrections involve the application of heavy and sophisticated equipment that you will probably have no access to either physically or financially. The big rigs and correction equipment necessary to realign heavily damaged areas are only found in the most sophisticated body shops.

If you have suffered heavy collision damage requiring radical realignment, it is best to find a good, reputable frame shop. When checking out the shop of your choice, make sure it has adequate equipment to do the necessary job *perfectly*. Stay away from gypsy "eyeballers" who do no more than straighten bent frames and measure axle-to-axle and assume that this will correct alignment problems. This obtuse method may appear adequate visually but is deceptive and in no way can correct alignment.

Alignment is particularly critical involving radical collision to the newer cars (X-bodies, etc.) in which the rack-and-pinion steering system is integrated into the body shell and the suspension separately secured on a subframe (or engine cradle). When the body shell and subframe get knocked out of alignment or out of square with each other, serious steering problems can occur. With the X-cars and all cars utilizing the Macpherson strut system, total alignment correction is *mandatory* to avoid erratic steering behavior.

Though the unitized cars can present a problem, this problem has been solved by one of the prominent manufacturers of frame and alignment equipment, Kansas Jack. The Kansas Jack Corporation is the prime innovator of the Lazer Beam Aligner™ system, which is tailored for solving complex problems inherent in Macpherson strut alignments as well as other alignment quirks of unitized body cars. When a unibody car gets hit, more damage can occur than is seen with the naked eye. A rear-end collision can cause damage up front. Even minor impacts to the unibody structure can affect strut alignment and steering.

The Lazer Beam Aligner™ offers total vehicle correction never before possible with conventional systems. Utilizing laser beams, this revolutionary and exacting system isolates damage anywhere on the vehicle and allows the technician to monitor and calibrate progress to the smallest degree as he is making corrections. The new system allows perfect squaring and alignment of body shells, axles, wheels, steering, and suspension to exacting factory specs. The "total correction" concept is the basis of the system.

The system can also locate the geometric center of a vehicle regardless of the extent of damage in order to allow either horizontal or vertical alignment with almost zero margin of error. Control points can be localized much more precisely and efficiently than with standard jigs. Datum lines are easily calculated in any area of the car — even in cases where original center lines are undeterminable.

Wheel alignment is another area in which the Lazer

Beam Aligner™excells. The system will pinpoint wheel runout and check camber, caster, strut angle, and strut pivot axis.

It is difficult to describe how unique and near-perfect this system is. With the laser aligner, problems

Fig. 15-1. The Kansas Jack Laser System. The elaborate equipment disassembles for easy storage.

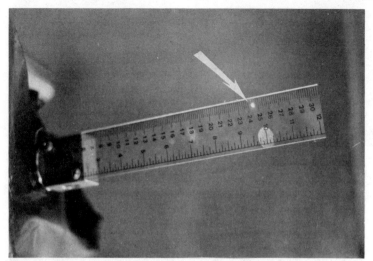

Fig. 15-2. Correct alignment specs were checked in order to determine proper attachment points etc., for proper front suspension alignment.

can be discovered and solved even if the vehicle control points are in the wrong place — the machine will determine proper factory locations.

No doubt you will agree that *this* is the proper way to achieve complete corrective alignment. Your main objective if you have collision alignment problems is to locate a Lazer system in your area. Information as to the locale of frame specialists utilizing the Lazer Beam Alignment™ system may be obtained from:

Kansas Jack Inc.
1101 West First
McPherson, KS 67460 (316) 241-0830

Figures 15-1 and 15-2 show only a part of a job in which a totaled-out Ferrari is resurrected, a feat that would have been scarcely conceivable without the Lazer Alignment system.

The operation was performed at The Body Shop, Pompano Beach, Florida, under the supervision of owner Mike Wright and assisted by K-J representative John Ames.

Repairing Fiberglass

Many automotive body components today are manufactured of fiberglass. These include header panels, headlight housings, and other integral parts that do not require the strength of steel.

In many cases they can be repaired so that when repainted the damaged area will not show — and in most instances the part will be stronger at the repair point than in the rest of the component.

To attain optimum strength, the torn or damaged piece should be reinforced on the inside or backside using resin-impregnated fiberglass cloth. One of the best medias for fiberglass repair is Evercoat fiberglass resin; it is heavy and does not tend to sag on vertical surfaces as much as other resins. Evercoat Marine Resin is also an excellent product. Both can be readily obtained at auto or marine shop suppliers.

Fiberglass cloth reinforcement is also recommended in Corvette repairs. Tears, gouges, and larger areas to be covered can then be filled in with Evercoat Vette Panel Adhesive and sanded smooth.

For smaller repairs, fiberglass tape is recommended. Fiberglass tape is actually fiberglass cloth in rolls about five inches wide. It is preferable to regular cloth; it

Fig. 16-1. Damage on fiberglass header panel.

is stronger, with a tighter knit, and is convenient to cut and lay over areas that need reinforcement.

Figures 16-1 through 16-6 show a typical fiberglass repair procedure on a common fiberglass automobile component — a front header panel, in this case from a Pontiac Grand Prix. Similar units are found on autos of other manufacturers.

In this example we tackle a tear to the side of the right headlight area (Fig. 16-1). In Fig. 16-2, notice that the tear is completely through, weakening and bending the damaged surface. The area must first be both realigned and strengthened; this will be done in the initial stage of the repair, which will be handled on the inside of the panel where it will be unobtrusive.

The section to be overlayed with resin-impregnated cloth is sanded with 80-grit sandpaper to promote positive adhesion between the resin and the panel inner surface. Next, the two edges to be joined are brought into proper alignment (Fig. 16-3). Here we use a Vise Grip, spanning the section to be repaired and the bolt lug inside the header. The Vise Grip screw adjustment is rotated until the two broken edges align as shown.

Then fiberglass cloth cut to the required size is saturated with catalyzed resin. When adding hardener to resin and mixing the two, follow the directions on the can *exactly*. (Don't mix more than is required, as resin is not cheap.) Avoid skin contact; the resin is messy, toxic, and its fumes should not be inhaled. Do this work in a well-ventilated area and use rubber

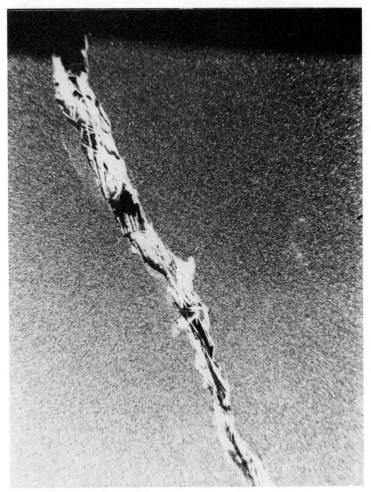

Fig. 16-2. Close up of crack.

Fig. 16-3. Aligning the torn segments.

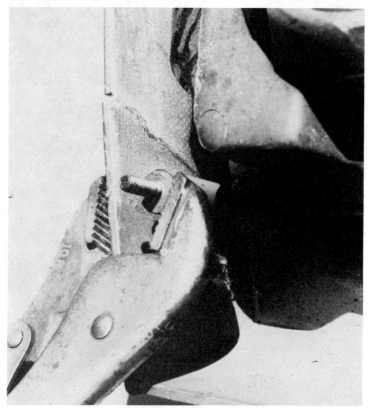

Fig. 16-4. Cloth is applied and smoothed down.

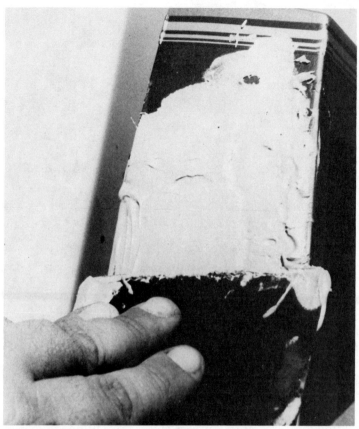

Fig. 16-5. Body filler is applied to the side opposite the cloth reinforced area.

gloves. Take your time in application; the resin does not set up quickly.

Build up the cloth layers slowly in an overlapping fashion. Three layers of fiberglass tape should suffice for adequate reinforcement. Figure 16-4 shows the resin-impregnated tape in place and smoothed out.

Allow about 24 hours for full curing, after which you can begin the second phase of the repair — filling in the gap on the outside of the header panel. For this job we use Evercoat Vette Panel Adhesive, which acts and is applied in the same fashion as Bondo. The filler is catalyzed, thoroughly mixed, and applied with a

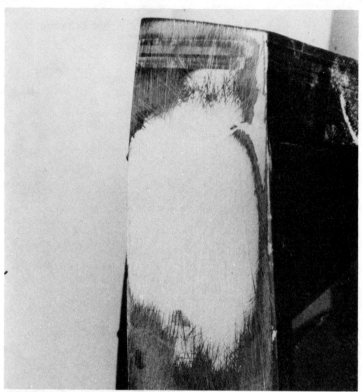

Fig. 16-6. Finished repair.

squeegee (Fig. 16-5). When cured, the filler is sanded down with a small rubber block and 80-grit sandpaper.

Figure 16-6 shows the repaired and finished header panel segment ready for priming, glazing, and painting.

Spray Equipment and Spraying Basics

The spray gun (production type) is a necessity for professional or do-it-yourself bodywork finishing. In finishing, it is used to apply the primer coats required for filling in body filler scratches and properly preparing the body repair surfaces for final painting. For spraying paint and paint refinishing, it is *the* tool; when used properly it can produce exotic paint jobs far superior to the factory finishes on new cars. To achieve flawless finishing and perfect painting, you *must* become proficient in the use of the production spray gun.

The spray gun is an easy tool to learn and master. Practice and good control habits can enable even the duffer to realize excellent or perfect paint jobs.

The production gun most commonly used in auto body work is the siphon-type gun with an external mix (air/fluid) air cap. One of the finer production guns of this type available today is the Sharpe 75. The Sharpe is an external mix gun with two control knobs—a standard setup. In an external mix siphon gun of this type, the air and paint combine outside the nozzle cap as shown in Fig. 17-1. The air forced out through the orifices in the "ears" (proturberances of the cap) and the fluid orifice draw out the liquid paint

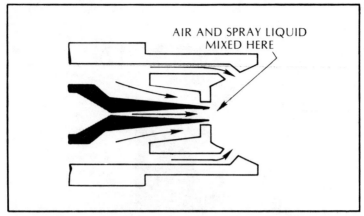

Fig. 17-1. The external mix configuration and how air and fluid combine. (courtesy Campbell-Hausfeld)

and allow it to atomize with air forced through the gun, spraying it in a controlled fan pattern. The shape of the spray pattern can be regulated by an external control knob, as can the amount of fluid flow.

Figure 17-2 shows a cutaway view of the Sharpe 75 and its working and control parts. At point A is the fan pattern control. This knob adjusts the width of the spray. Turned fully outward (counterclockwise), the gun will provide a large oval fan spray pattern. Turned all the way in (clockwise) the pattern is more concentrated and circular. Large, oval patterns are necessary for large area coverage; smaller, round patterns are better for small and more confined coverage.

Knob B meters the fluid flow; the farther outward it is revolved, the more paint flows. Item C is the trigger; pulling it back begins the spraying operation. At various metering locations from full out to full in, the trigger also aids in varying air-fluid combinations. Item D is the air cap or nozzle. The air intake is situated in the handle at E; F is the fluid siphon inlet.

HANDLING THE SPRAY GUN

Although learning to manipulate a spray gun is a simple task, it is a good idea to fully familiarize yourself with its operation before tackling an actual refinishing job. Practice spraying on discarded metal panels or cardboard. A half-hour of preliminary spray gun practice will enable you to get the feel of the gun and put you well on the way to tackling a first, simple job.

The best way to gain expertise is to first experiment on test surfaces. The working distance from gun to surface should be between six and twelve inches, depending on the paint flow and density of the atomized spray. Trigger the gun and examine the spray coat. If it is too fine or weak, turn down the air pressure or open up the fluid control knob. If the spray is too

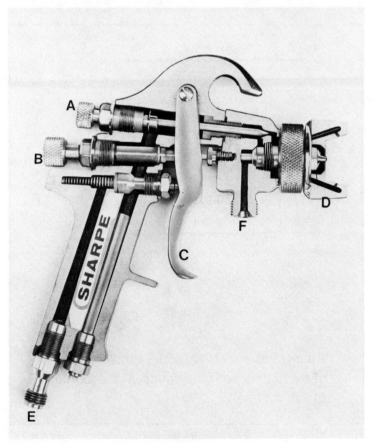

Fig. 17-2. Cutaway of the Sharp 75 spray gun.

coarse or dense, close down on the fluid knob.

Always keep the gun in constant side-to-side movement while spraying. If you don't, the paint will accumulate in one spot and eventually begin to sag or run. For wide area coverage, use a wide spray (oval) pattern. For small areas, or close and irregular surface work, use the more confined round pattern. When switching from an oval to a round spray pattern, the fluid metering control knob must be readjusted. Whichever way the pattern and emission are adjusted, remember that as the width of the fan and emission of fluid are increased, the spray particles become heavier. A heavy, hard-to-control pattern will not give optimum

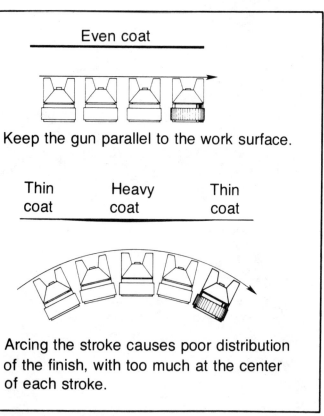

Fig. 17-3. Proper spraygun-to-surface manipulation. (courtesy Campbell-Hausfeld)

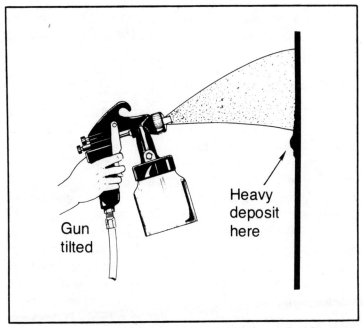

Fig. 17-4. Problems caused by tilting the gun in operation. (courtesy Campbell-Hausfeld)

results. The most workable spray/density pattern is one that handles easily while allowing sufficient coverage.

Side-to-side spray gun manipulation and speed also govern the appearance of the final paint finish. The speed at which the gun is moved controls the evenness of paint application. Moving too fast does not allow the paint to cover properly and may result in a grainy finish. Moving too slowly will allow the paint to build up too much, causing sags or runs.

When spraying, the gun must be kept strictly parallel and at a 90-degree angle to the working surface. Always flex your wrist at the end of each stroke to allow the gun to remain parallel to the working surface. Never spray in an arcing or curving side stroke —a common mistake of the beginning spray painter. Arcing the stroke allows uneven coating and overspray deposit at the end of the stroke (Fig. 17-3). Furthermore, if the gun is tilted up or down, more paint will build up at one edge of the stroke (Fig. 17-4). Correct triggering must become a habit and will help build your skill as a spray painter.

OVERLAPPING STROKES

When spraying large areas, your strokes must be overlapped to build up an even overall color film. First make the initial stroke covering the length of the area to be painted. Start the stroke with the trigger off; at the edge of the work area, pull the trigger and spray a full stroke. Stop the trigger action at the end of the work area *while the gun is still in motion.* Apply the next stroke in the same fashion coming back in the opposite direction, but allow this stroke to overlap the first one by about 50 percent. Continue on in this fashion until the work area is fully and evenly covered. The aiming point for each consecutive stroke should be the bottom edge of the preceding stroke (Fig. 17-5). This method is especially effective when painting with automotive lacquers and acrylic enamels.

SPRAY GUN MAINTENANCE

Spray gun maintenance is critical but easily performed. Always keep the spray gun *meticulously* clean.

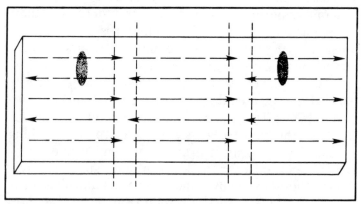

Fig. 17-5. Proper overlapping technique. (courtesy Campbell-Hausfeld)

Clean it after use by spraying thinner through it until *all* traces of color disappear. Then remove the spray cap and immerse it in thinner. All orifices should be cleaned; if paint buildup or clogging occurs, it can be reamed out with a small pin or needle.

Exercise safety precautions when spraying paint or cleaning guns. *Never* smoke or work near open flames while spraying as automotive paints and thinners are highly volatile. *Always* spray in a well-ventilated area. *Always* wear a proper respirator to filter out toxic fumes; these are hazardous to your lungs and could prove fatal over prolonged periods.

TROUBLESHOOTING SPRAY GUNS

No matter how careful you are, at some time or another you will encounter aberrations in spray patterns or faulty operation of the gun. Figure 17-6 details some of the common problems and how to avoid or correct them.

THE TOUCH-UP OR JAMB GUN

Scaled-down versions of the production gun are also available. These specialized guns (Fig. 17-7) are specifically designed for small area coverage and confined areas. These guns provide a smaller spray pattern (usually from one quarter inch to three inches); they work and adjust in the same manner as production spray guns. They are particularly suited to spraying around lights and crevices and for painting door jambs.

AIR COMPRESSORS

Compressors for spraying paint need not be as powerful as those required for heavy-duty body shop tools. A 1½-horsepower unit is more than adequate for the weekend mechanic (Fig. 17-8).

Since proper working air pressure is crucial for good results, a regulator must be used to obtain the correct pressures (for automotive paints, between 35

CONDITION	CAUSE	CORRECTION
 RIGHT	Correct Normal Pattern.	No Correction Necessary

WRONG
Heavy Top Or Bottom Pattern
	1. Dirty or damaged air cap.
	
	2. Dirty or damaged fluid tip.
		1. Rotate air cap 180°.
		
		  A. If pattern follows air cap, problem is in air cap. Clean and inspect. If pattern is not corrected, replacement is necessary.
		
		  B. If pattern does not follow the air cap, the problem is in the fluid tip. Clean and inspect the tip for dried paint, dirt or damage. If the pattern is not corrected, replacement is necessary.

 WRONG Split Pattern	1. Air pressure too high for material viscosity being sprayed.	1. Reduce air pressure. 2. Increase material viscosity. 3. Pattern may also be corrected by narrowing fan size with spray width adjuster control knob.

Fig. 17-6. Spray gun test patterns. (courtesy Sharpe Manufacturing)

138

CONDITION	CAUSE	CORRECTION
WRONG	1. Dirty or distorted air horn holes. 2. Complete blockage of one air horn hole.	1. Rotate air cap 180°. A. If pattern follows air cap, clean and inspect the air horn holes. If horn holes are distorted replacement is necessary.
WRONG Gun Spitting	1. Air getting into paint stream somewhere. *EXAMPLE:* Same symptoms as a siphon cup running out of paint.	1. Check and tighten fluid needle packing nut. 2. Tighten fluid tip. 3. Check fluid tip seat for damage. 4. Check siphon tube for crack. 5. Check for poor gun to cup seating.
Air Back Pressuring Into Cup	Excessive Air Blowing Back Into Cup.	1. Tighten fluid tip. 2. Check fluid tip seat. 3. Check for damaged fluid seat on tip or seat in gun head.

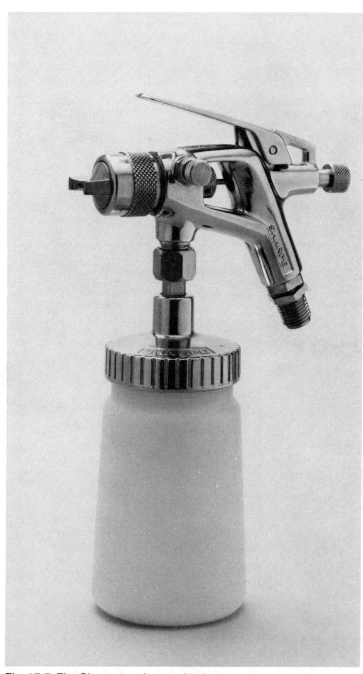

Fig. 17-7. The Sharpe touch-up or jamb gun.

Fig. 17-8. The Campbell-Hausfeld Power Pro--an excellent 1 1/2-hp unit that is ideal for the Saturday spray painter.

Fig. 17-9. Small regulator valves, such as produced by Sharpe Mfg., mount on the spray gun and are always in easy reach.

and 50 psi). One handy unit is the small and inexpensive regulator shown in Fig. 17-9. It mounts directly under the spray gun air inlet, making it readily accessible for changing air pressure at any time.

Prepping and Painting

Although final painting is the shortest and quickest phase of the refinishing procedure, it is also the most critical, being the most obvious and eye-catching part of the body beautification operation. A most important factor to remember is that new or repair paint finishes are not always applied over identical surfaces or bases; hence, prepping approaches will differ and must be handled appropriately. You will encounter several — or possibly all — of them at one time or another.

BARE STEEL

One surface that is ideal but rarely encountered by the spot or overall painter is bare metal. The ideal approach for flawless painting involves getting the working surface down to bare metal. This is done by one of three methods, depending on which is the most applicable to the situation encountered:

- ■ Chemical stripping.
- ■ Sandblasting.
- ■ Hand-sanding or machine grinding.

Chemical stripping involves brushing on a paint-

Fig. 18-1. A razor blade scraper can be quite useful for removing paint quickly and effectively.

dissolving solution that eats into and loosens existing paint and primer films. Residue and bubbled-up paint are then scraped away with a putty knife or paint scraper. Repeated applications may be necessary depending on the hardness and thickness of the existing paint. Commercial paint strippers are available at all paint and hardware suppliers for this purpose.

Sandblasting is the best method of paint removal and one of the prime functions of the sandblaster. (I consider it a *necessary* tool for the do-it-yourselfer, as I have stated elsewhere in this book.) Though a bit messy (sand gets blown all over the place), sandblasting *thoroughly* cleans the bare metal and gives it a "tooth" that is a great asset in securing prime and paint coatings. A number of sandblasting abrasive media are available: 30- and 70-grit sand, aluminum oxide, and glass bead. The more common 30-grit sand is adequate for all sandblasting situations you are likely to encounter, and is also the cheapest. Proper sandblasting technique is described in Chapter 14.

Hand-sanding or grinding is another inexpensive and effective paint removing alternative. Hand-sanding involves much time and labor using 36-grit coarse paper; I don't enthusiastically recommend it due to the excessive elbow grease and time factors involved. A razor blade scraper (Fig. 18-1) is a great hand-paint removal tool but its use also involves a great deal of time.

Machine grinding is an excellent method and is best performed with the DA (dual orbital sander). As seen in Fig. 18-2, the air sander is used in this instance in

Fig. 18-2. The DA equipped with a heavy-grit sanding disk will effectively remove old paint quickly. It is also excellent for feathering body plastic. (courtesy Chicago Pneumatic)

the non-offset mode (revolving in a strictly circular motion). The applicable sanding disk here is 80-grit, which will tear off old paint film quickly and completely.

Once you have gotten down to bare metal, you should use some approved method to properly condition the metal for rust inhibition and proper adhesion of primer and paint. The conditioning of bare metal is usually undertaken with special chemicals that contain phosphoric acid. Treatment with metal prep conditioners dissolves oils, oxidizing agents, and other contaminants that may be present in the metal. As the phosphate treatment is washed and scrubbed into the metal, the metal is etched and oxidation is terminated and eliminated. This washing/etching action is extremely effective for optimum primer adhesion. After its application, the chemical must be washed away with water and the bare metal *immediately* primed or sealed to avoid further corrosion.

Several excellent metal prep solutions are available in auto paint stores. For most automotive steels, Fibre Glass Evercoat's Feather Prep or Dupont 5717S Metal Conditioner are excellent. For hot- and cold-rolled steel that will be exposed to severe conditions, Dupont 224S Steel Conversion Coating produces a high degree of corrosion resistance and optimum paint adhesion. For aluminum, Dupont 226S Conversion Coating is recommended; it should be applied after flushing with Dupont 225S Aluminum Cleaner. For galvanized iron and zinc metal compounds, another prepping agent is available: Dupont 227S.

Once the bare metal has been properly prepped and treated, priming the surface is the next step. Primers are *essential* — not only to coat bare metal, but also to promote positive paint adhesion. Though many paints will adhere to untreated or unprimed metal surfaces, they will in time tend to become brittle and lose elasticity, which helps prevent proper bonding. After conditioning, *all* metals should be prime-coated to promote optimum adhesion as well as fill in minor flaws and scratches. The filling properties of primer help to achieve smooth working surfaces prior to color-coating.

Lacquer-based primers are usually best suited for painting over common bare metal. Build up a thick film by spraying with a standard production gun — preferably one with a large paint orifice, since primer is thicker and more viscous than paint. In many cases, repeated coating may be required along with between-coat sanding with 220-grit dry paper to realize a perfectly smooth and scratch-free working surface.

Mix primers according to the recommendations on the can and always use quick-drying thinners. Apply lacquer primers in heavy, wet coats; thin, dry coats do not adhere to metal as well and promote poor adhesion. Primers, properly applied and mixed with the fastest flashing thinners, can be sanded 30 minutes after the final coat, though a longer drying time is even more desirable to allow proper shrinkage and adequate solvent evaporation.

PREPPING ALUMINUMS

Some auto components such as hoods and deck lids may be made of aluminum. Aluminum parts can be identified with a magnet, which will not stick to aluminum as it will to steel. In preparing aluminum for priming, hand- or machine-sand with 180-grit dry paper. Do not apply excessive pressure; aluminum is softer than most metals and not as resistant to abrasion. Prime aluminum in the same manner as steel but instead of the standard acrylic lacquer metal primer, use zinc chromate primer, which is expressly formulated for proper and positive adhesion on aluminum.

PREPPING GALVANIZED PANELS

In the past few years, automobile manufacturers have leaned toward the use of galvanized metal in rocker panels, rear extension panels, cowl panels, and even deck lids. Some older vehicles sport panels that are galvanized on both sides, while many of the newer models contain sheet steel galvanized on only one side. Good paint adhesion is a common problem with galvanized metal and certain steps must be taken for paint to remain on galvanized panels for extended periods of time.

Refinishing a galvanized panel that has been factory-painted requires the *complete* removal of paint. This is usually done with a razor blade scraper. Then sand the bare galvanized surface completely with 180-grit sandpaper to smooth out and remove all scratches and scuff up the surface. Thoroughly clean and coat the galvanized surface with the appropriate galvanized metal conditioner (Dupont 227S or equivalent). Wash off excess prep medium and wipe dry with a clean cloth, then spray with zinc phosphate primer specially formulated for galvanized metal. This step is *extremely* important and this type of primer is universally marketed by all automotive paint companies. After the primer has completely dried (a 24-hour period is advised) the primed panel should be scuffed using fine sandpaper to smooth out the primer coat — if the paint to be used is enamel, use 400-grit sandpaper; if the top coat will be lacquer, 600-grit sandpaper is recommended.

By following the above instructions exactly you can achieve a perfect finish on galvanized metal that will last for years.

PREPPING FIBERGLASS

Prepping Corvettes and other fiberglass-bodied cars involves procedures similar to those for metal along with extreme caution using strong chemicals and abrasive machine tools. Eighty-grit sandpaper is the most coarse you can safely use, as the softer fiberglass surface scratches easily. Use only recommended paint strippers or chemicals with fiberglass, since the "hotter" strippers can attack and melt the resin.

Feather Fill, a two-part catalyzed primer, is great for fiberglass; it produces a durable, hard dried surface and powerful adhesion. Hardened Feather Fill surfaces are best hand-sanded with 100-grit sandpaper. Never wet-sand Feather Fill or problems will appear and mar or damage paint overcoatings. Standard acrylic-based primers are also suited to prepping fiberglass surfaces.

PAINTING OVER FACTORY AND REPAINTED SURFACES

You will often have occasion to paint over a factory paint job or a repainted area. Some special procedures here will permit the next paint coat you apply to adhere properly without affecting the paint film underneath.

Most cars today are factory-painted with baked-on acrylic enamel. When applying new paint over these hardened finishes, you must properly prepare them to promote proper adhesion.

Whether you are repainting in lacquer or enamel, a sealer is just about mandatory between factory and recoat finishes. Sealers for use over factory paint are mainly designed to provide positive adhesion of consecutive coatings. To assure good bonding, I advise the use of Ditzler 1947 clear sealer in all situations except some of the GM water-based enamels. These are designated by the letter W after the paint code number found on the color plate under the hood. Water-based acrylic enamels should be sealed with R-M 811 sealer, which is specifically formulated for this purpose.

Most all sealers come as clear or tinted primer/sealer versions that also prime as they seal. Sealers are formulated with special resins that don't allow common lacquer and enamel solvents to react or fail in maintaining adhesion with sensitive undercoats. Some sealers are dual-purpose preventing solvent penetration and at the same time preventing abnormal reaction between over and undercoats.

Acrylic lacquers (which contain more active solvents than enamels) should not be applied haphazardly over porous finishes. However, when good sealer is applied before lacquer repainting and a less-penetrating lacquer thinner utilized, the lacquer will not tend to harm the undersurface as rapidly. In most cases, the protective intermediate sealer will prevent solvent penetration that can wrinkle or lift the undercoating (especially if the undercoating consists of an enamel or non-hardened acrylic enamel film).

Before sealing and priming, all surfaces should be well-sanded with 320- or 400-grit sandpaper. Apply sealers according to the instructions provided on their respective labels.

PRIMING

Another procedure sometimes added after sealing is priming. In most cases, lacquer primers are selected (for their quick-drying characteristics), thinned with non-penetrating quick-drying solvents. Primers are universally used in spot repair situations over body filler and putty work. Before priming, the surface should be smoothed and feathered to minimize surface scratches. A dual orbital sander works best here with a 220-grit sanding disk attached (Fig. 18-3). Surface coating the area with successive coats of primer (until all scratches are eliminated and filled in), followed by finish hand-sanding with 220- or 320-grit dry sandpaper will properly prepare the surface for final paint coating.

When priming over repaint enamel finishes, use extreme caution. Paint "dry" and not "wet" and do not allow the solvent used to penetrate the enamel film or lifting will occur.

Occasionally you will come across undersurfaces so sensitive that no amount of caution or lacquer application precautionary techniques will inhibit wrinkling. In these cases, abandon the acrylic lacquer primer and use instead one of the new "miracle" water-borne primers that are specially concocted for use over sensi-

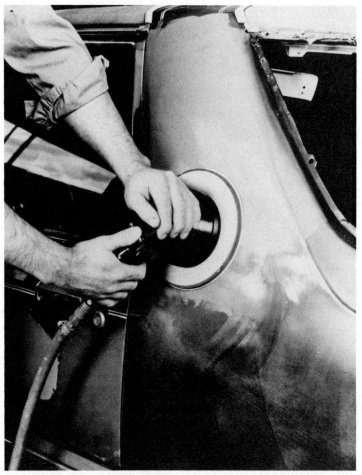

Fig. 18-3. Feathering out repaint areas with the DA and 220-grit sanding disk. (courtesy Chicago Pneumatic)

tive enamel coatings. One of the best of these is R-M 806 Barrier Coat Water-Borne Primer Sealer. With R-M 806 you need not worry about highly sensitive (to lacquer) undercoats or possible damage to the undersurface. R-M 806 will completely eliminate swelling and lifting.

The 806 must be applied with care. It is very slow-drying; quick repetitive coats may cause runs.

Once the proper drying time has passed, 806 can be

sanded easily (but lightly) and topcoated with any type of finish without fear of undercoat damage.

CHOOSING PAINT

Today there is a variety of automotive refinishing paints and systems. Five types prevail: *acrylic lacquer, acrylic enamel, nitrocellulose lacquer, alkyd enamel,* and *urethane enamels.* Breaking it down further, the aforementioned paints can be categorized as *lacquers* or *enamels.*

Enamels (including acrylic enamels and urethanes) require painting under ideal conditions. They are slower-drying, hence can pick up dust and dirt easily. If improperly applied, enamels tend to run. They are dangerous healthwise, and cause adverse respiratory reactions. The use of a proper protective mask is *strongly* recommended. The pro factors for enamels and acrylic enamels and urethanes include a high-gloss finish (requiring no buffing) and superb coating resiliency. Enamels should be sprayed in a completely dust-free area (preferably a commercial booth) and under optimum ventilation conditions. Enamel or acrylic enamel painting is not recommended for the weekend do-it-yourselfer. Urethane enamels, the most exotic paints, also carry exotic prices.

For the weekend dabbler or part-time bodyworker, acrylic lacquer is the best paint to use. It is fast-drying and the ideal choice for spot and partial repair work. Final coats can be blended into the undercoat with a thinned color/clear solution; this allows the repaired area color to fade into the undercoat, minimizing slight discrepancies in color shading and hue.

For overall (complete car) painting, lacquer is again the desired medium. Its quick-drying quality allows less dust to embed itself into the film. Lacquer can be effectively sprayed in a garage — even with the door open, provided you do not choose a windy day for your painting.

Three basic thinners are used with acrylic lacquer systems. One is a quick-drying solvent suitable for primers, base coatings, and spot repairs (also for cold-weather, minimal-humidity conditions). The second is an all-purpose medium dry solvent used for general painting conditions. The third is a slow-drying thinner that is highly penetrating and offers high-gloss finish. Slow-drying thinners are also recommended for use under excessively warm, humid conditions.

A fourth medium, only used when needed to control blushing and finish gloss, is *retarder* or *reflow solvent*. Blushing and gloss inhibition can occur under high-humidity conditions. What causes the lacquer to blush and chalk is rapid cooling (inherent in faster thinners) due to accelerated evaporation. This allows moisture to become entrapped in the film, consequently causing a hazed finish.

The following solvent recommendations are set forth for the do-it-yourselfer.

■ Use a quick-drying thinner for priming, spot repair, and low temperature conditions.

■ Use a general-medium, all-purpose thinner for overall painting under stable weather conditions.

■ Use a slow-drying thinner for a high-gloss finish and for final topcoats in excessively humid surroundings.

■ Keep retarder on hand in the event blushing occurs and to further lengthen drying times in order to promote high gloss. Retarders should be used *only* when needed. Too much retarder will affect the drying time, possibly causing a slow-drying paint film to sag or run.

Paint thinning ratios for lacquer and solvents are generally 150 percent (one part lacquer to one-and-a-half parts thinner). In general, lacquer/solvent ratios run from 1:1 to 1:2 depending on the viscosity of the lacquer (which can differ between manufacturers) and the thinner (slow or fast) used. The best advice is to follow

Fig. 18-4. The Binks Organic Vapor paint mask. Equipped with the 40-127 filters, it cuts down the respiratory hazards involved in enamel and lacquer painting.

the directions on the labels of the various products.

Proper spraying and spraygun technique for lacquer (and other paints) is presented in detail in Chapter 17.

When spraying lacquers, enamels, or urethanes, always — *religiously* — use a mask — not just a dust mask, but an organic vapor type such as shown in Fig. 18-4.

COLOR MATCHING

One of the most common problems in spot or sectional painting is color matching. In most cases new paint will not match up to old, no matter how accurate the formulation. Modifications in shading and hue will most likely have to be made to the repainted area. When you buy paint, always specify "factory pack," which comes closest in conforming to the original color. The best color match factory packs seem to be the R – M brand. Ditzler is another good factory pack choice.

Before spot painting, compound a small area of the original color to obtain an accurate color for matching. Try to match the repainting color to the old paint (and this is not too easy for the neophyte). Check the original color for *depth*; see if it is lighter or darker than the fresh paint. Check for *cast* differences to see if the paint should be redder, bluer, greener, etc. Check for *cleanliness*, which also affects color. In some cases, new paint will have to be tinted "dirtier" or castwise to match the original color.

As you tint the paint, make tests. Use a paint stick; dip it into the fresh paint and allow the paint to dry on it. Then place the new *dry* paint against the old finish for a color check.

Spraygun technique can also be used for adjustments in color variation. When changing from darker to lighter using spraygun techniques, keep in mind that you also tend to change the cast as well.

SPRAY GUN COLOR ADJUSTMENT

Spray gun distance is a factor that has an effect on color. Increasing the distance between the gun and surface (for a dryer spray) will make the paint coat lighter. Decreasing the distance (wet coating) will make the paint coat darker. Side-to-side motion of the gun will also affect shading. A fast application speed will allow lighter coloration; a slower speed produces a darker one.

Fluid flow adjustment can also be used for color correction. Decreasing fluid flow will lighten coloration; increasing fluid flow will darken it. Increased air pressure likewise will lighten color; decreased air pressure will darken it.

The choice of thinners can also serve to manipulate color. Faster thinners give lighter coloration; slower thinners produce darker coloration. Increasing the amount of thinner will lighten color; decreasing the amount of thinner serves to darken color.

If the color must be tinted (redder, bluer, greener, yellower), you will have to use proper toning agents. These are available from the same sources that provide your paint. The proper matching of colors can only be achieved by experimentation with color mixing and spraying.

COLOR MATCHING METALLICS

Color matching of metallics is even trickier than matching solid colors. Again, use "factory pack" colors for closest matches. The most important factor in matching metallics is mixing. Make sure the paint is *fully* mixed so that the metal particles are properly and fully suspended in the solution.

Unique to metallic painting is an adverse condition known as *flip-flop*. A color match is achieved when the section is viewed from one direction. If the color changes when you change the viewing angle, you have a flip-flop condition.

This problem occurs frequently in polychrome (metallic) paints and involves the suspension of the metallic flakes and the way that they reflect light back to the observer. This condition will happen more often with lighter poly colors.

Spray technique will help in controlling or eliminating flip-flop. Wet spraying will darken the overall appearance when viewed directly and lighten it when viewed at an angle. Dry spraying produces the opposite effect. A proper compromise should be reached by gun manipulation until the repainted area corresponds to the adjacent color area with a more harmonizing metallic/tone color balance. Tinting may also be necessary for proper color harmony and the same standard toners and experimentation procedures listed above for solid colors are advised. I strongly recommend that you obtain an excellent metallic color matching chart provided by Acme and available through paint sources that carry the Acme Automotive Finish line. It's called the Acme Metallic Color Tinting guide and shows how to match standard metallic colors in hue and cast.

MASKING

A few words should be said about masking, as it is required in all spot and repaint situations to control overspray.

For chrome and moldings, use a good grade ¾ inch or 2 inch masking tape; 3M fine-grade is the best. For larger areas, use masking paper in conjunction with masking tape. A good cheap substitute for masking paper is newspaper, which everyone has unlimited access to. Cover all areas that are not to be painted completely and neatly (see Fig. 18-5).

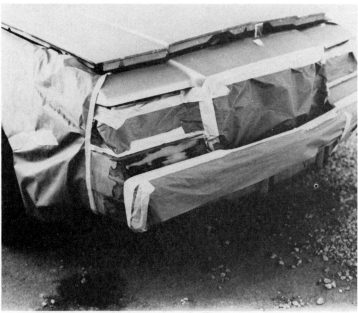

Fig. 18-5. Here only a hood and header panel top are to be painted so the adjacent areas are masked off with tape and paper.

COMMON PAINT PROBLEMS

There are many common aberrations that can occur (particularly for the beginning painter); these can cause flaws to appear directly or indirectly if care and some precautions are not taken. The following are some of the most common problems and how to get around them if they should occur.

Sags and Runs: Runs generally occur because of inexperience: The beginner lays on too much paint, the film becomes too thick and heavy to support itself, and the wet paint sags or runs in rivulets that appear unsightly and ruin the overall surface. There are also a number of contributing causes to this problem: Holding the spray gun too close to the surface while painting will cause an excessive buildup of paint. Too-low air pressure will prevent sufficient atomization of the spray and this can also result in running. Laying on successive coats without allowing proper drying time between coats will promote sags. All these factors can be minimized or eliminated by proper use of the spray gun and proper mixing of paint and thinner.

If runs or sags *do* occur, allow the marred film to *fully* dry and then sand it down until the runs are feathered into the surface coat. If necessary, apply a few cover coats of paint after sanding.

Orange Peel: This common occurrence is aptly named because it resembles the surface of an orange. Improper gun adjustment and improper thinners can cause orange peeling from minor to major degrees. Under-reduction of paint is a common cause, followed by using an improper thinner or improper pressure. Follow the paint manufacturer's mixing ratio recommendations or spray a test sheet of metal to ensure that your paint is properly thinned. Make sure the air pressure at the gun does not exceed 50 pounds. To minimize orange peel in all painted surfaces, utilize a slow-drying thinner, which will allow better flowout of the paint film. The remedy for orange peel is simple: Sand the irregular surface until it is smooth, then buff it out with rubbing compound to restore the gloss. You can also recoat after sanding.

Fish Eyes: Fish eyes are very common, particularly when the surface to be painted is not *completely* free of oil films or silicone contaminants found in auto waxes. Fish eyes occur in the form of circles or oil streaks; in most cases the crater-like "eyes" allow the undercolor to show through. If fish eyes occur, allow the marred areas to dry and then sand them down. Follow this with a thorough wash-down with a wax and grease remover such as Prep-Sol, Clesol, or Ditzler 330. If necessary, add a few drops of Marson Smoothie to the paint; this is only recommended as a last resort since the fish eye killer cuts down gloss and can inhibit good paint film adhesion. The best measure to take to inhibit fish eyes is thorough washing and degreasing of the surface prior to painting.

Peeling and Lifting: This is recognized by the separation of the newly applied paint film and the sensitive affected undercoat from the metal or undersurface. It may also appear as a wrinkled or prune-puckered finish, and will happen if acrylic lacquer is applied over synthetic enamel or uncured acrylic enamel. To prevent wrinkling or lifting, try not to apply acrylic lacquers over sensitive incompatible paint films. If you must, then spray on a sealer prior to color recoating to act as a protective buffer between the sensitive undersurface and the "hotter" overcoating. If lifting does occur, the surface must be resanded, sealed, and repainted.

Film Sheet Lifting: Not to be confused with the aforementioned lifting, this is confined to the peeling off in sheets of the dried paint film. It is due to poor adhesion, and almost always takes place when acrylic lacquer is shot over factory-baked hardened acrylic enamel with little or improper preparation of the surface to be repainted. The problem here is physical but not chemical adhesion; the overcoating does not grab onto or fuse with the factory paint. In cases of this kind the paint will peel off in sheets, or can be pulled off with tape stuck on the surface and yanked. To prevent this problem, sand all factory finishes with 400 wet-or-dry sandpaper and spray on two to three coats of sealer before painting.

Blistering: Swelled areas resembling blisters under the human skin but well-dispersed and numerous, this reaction may be caused by trapped solvents reacting, painting over rusty or oily surfaces, or moisture from air lines blown onto the surface and entrapped in the paint film. To prevent blistering, thoroughly remove *all* rust from surfaces to be painted, drain air lines of moisture frequently, and avoid the use of rapid-drying thinners when temperatures are high. The fix for existing blisters is sanding and refinishing the blistered areas.

Cracking and Checking: This problem is similar in appearance to shattered glass and can occur if precautions are not taken. It is more prevalent with lacquers than other coating mediums. The causes are many: improper drying time prior to recoating; repeated extreme temperature (weather) changes after the paint has dried; intermixing of thinners (types and brands); recoating a previously cracked finish; thinner attacking the surface of a cured lacquer; excessive use of retarder in lacquers; too thick a lacquer coating; ingredients of paint improperly mixed. This aberration may be disastrous and cannot be remedied other than by removing the cracked paint by sanding it *all* off, then repriming and repainting the area.

Blushing: Blushing or chalking happens when painting lacquer in high heat or excessive humidity condi-

Fig. 18-6. Final buffing to bring up surface gloss on lacquer repaint surface. (courtesy Chicago Pneumatic)

tions. It is easily recognized by its chalky white cast or dulling of the partial or overall finish. To avoid this problem, use a slow-drying thinner or add retarder to the paint. If chalking does occur, repaint with the same color using a better thinner balance.

FINAL FINISHING

Final finishing for lacquer paint involves buffing and polishing. Lightly wet-sand the surface with 600-grit paper. Then apply rubbing compound with a buffer until the finish is brought up to a high gloss (Fig. 18-6). A final polishing with Liquid Ebony polish will eliminate buff scratches and impart a glasslike appearance to the repainted surface.

Cosmetic Additives

Outer cosmetics can be considered "additive body-work" and are usually applied to individualize or customize an existing car. Decor additions can be major or minor accessories, removable or permanently secured. A number of aesthetic enhancements are listed in this chapter for the weekend mechanic who wishes to enhance the overall looks of his vehicle.

MOLDINGS

Moldings serve as protective as well as decorative add-ons. If you want to add moldings to a car when none are present, they can be purchased from an automotive dealer. Specify car model, year, color, and type desired.

Moldings are easy to apply. First strike a line using a carpenter's chalk striker (Fig. 19-1) to assure straight placement. Peel away the protective film to expose the adhesive backing (Fig. 19-2). Then pressure-fix the molding, using the chalk line as a guide (Fig. 19-3).

STRUCTURAL BODY ADDITIVES

This category includes spoilers, wings, flares,

Fig. 19-1. A chalk line is struck for alignment, the first step in adding a molding.

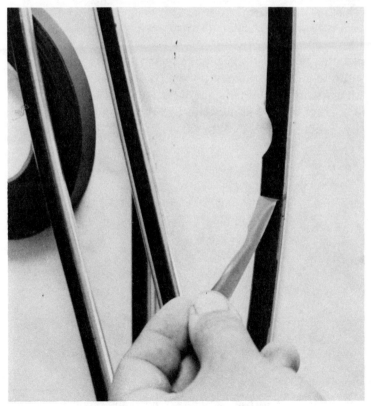

Fig. 19-2. Backing is peeled from molding adhesive.

Fig. 19-3. Molding is press-fitted into place.

scoops, and so on. Spoilers are available from the automobile manufacturers as well as a host of specialty firms, some of which cater to specific makes of cars.

Figure 19-4 shows the Kaminari Package (offered by Fiber Designs of Brea, California) formulated as

Fig. 19-4. The Kaminari Package designed and produced by Erik Cutter. (courtesy Fiber Designs)

replacement packages for Datsun Z and ZX automobiles. The Kaminari Package features replacement front fenders and integrated air dam; the fenders come complete with inner stiffness, inner wheel wells, and headlight mounting brackets. All parts replace the factory items with simple bolt-on installation. This would make an excellent weekend project for the Z buff, and similar packages are available from Eckler for Corvettes. A host of scoops and spoilers are available for many other popular street machine types.

STRIPES

Many striping materials are marketed, from wide racing stripes to decorative OEM-type pinstripes. Stick-on types can be found in standard and specialty auto supply shops. They are easy to apply and really dress up otherwise drab exterior. An extensive line of custom striping decor is marketed by Pro Stripe; a descriptive brochure may be obtained from:

> Spartan Plastics
> Box 67
> Holt, Michigan 48842

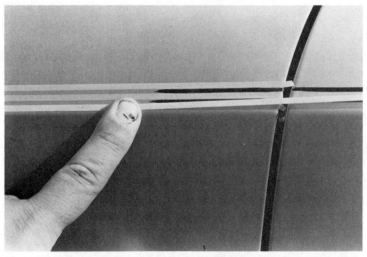

Fig. 19-5. Stripe masking is applied with 3M fine line plastic tape.

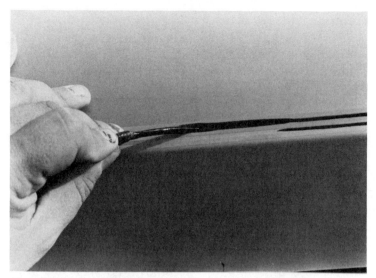

Fig. 19-6. Paint is applied with dagger brush between tape.

You may want to apply hand-painted stripes but not have any pinstriping expertise. I have found an easy and effective way to get around this. Using 3M fine-line plastic tape (⅛ inch), I mask off my lines as shown in Fig. 19-5. Then I apply the paint stripe with a striping

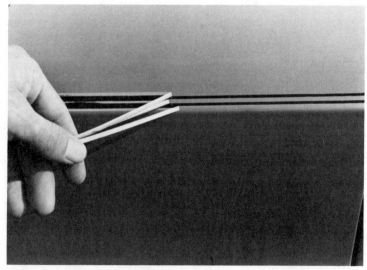

Fig. 19-7. Masking tape is peeled away.

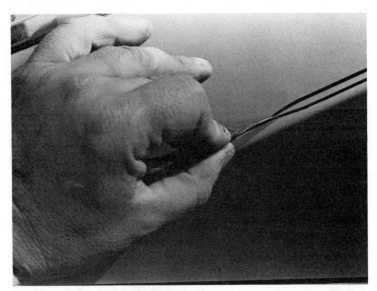

Fig. 19-8. Points are added freehand.

brush and block enamel (Fig. 19-6). Then the tape is peeled (Fig. 19-7), leaving perfect lines. These are then joined freehand in a point (Fig. 19-8). Figure 19-9 shows the finished professional looking job.

An even easier masking method that gives the same

Fig. 19-9. Completed hand stripping.

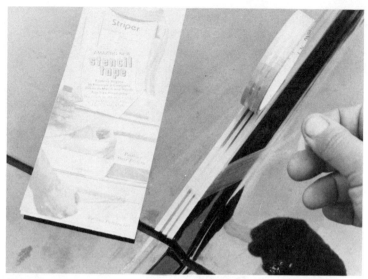

Fig. 19-10. Pre-spaced masking mediums are also available. Tape is applied and tacked and top tape film removed after tape alignment.

results involves pre-spaced stencil tape as shown in Fig. 19-10.

CUSTOM PAINTING

Custom painting is the ultimate way to go design-wise but should be attempted only after you are well-versed in spraygun manipulation.

Specialty paints — pearls, candies, and flakes — are available from such companies as Ditzler, Metalflake, and Aero Lac, and are available at some auto paint suppliers.

Sources for
Materials, Tools, and Parts

Most of the tooling and body shop products discussed throughout this manual are readily available to all weekend mechanics, usually within an average shopping distance.

In this chapter we will list some services and sources and try to advise you of the best ways to obtain bodywork necessities.

BODY PARTS

The auto salvage yard (also known as the junkyard) is a good one-stop shopping source for used parts — which are more economical and sometimes as good as new ones. Body parts (quarter panels, fenders, etc.), are not subjected to as much abuse as mechanical or engine parts, so there is no wear or age factor involved. Some cars in a yard may have rust-ridden parts, but careful selection and examination will almost always get you parts that are in good condition.

The better salvage yards are well-inventoried and parts are presorted and removed from incoming wrecks and usually marked and stocked for easy access. Some yards may still require you to remove the part you want, so bring the necessary tools with you. You will also find it cheaper to do your own salvage than to have the yard manager assign the task to one of the yard boys; a small labor charge may be tacked on. Yards specializing in certain makes or types of cars usually charge more per part, but they are also more likely to have a specific part for the types of autos they specialize in. Learn how to visit and examine the local yards. See how the prices vary and which yards are the most reasonable or best-stocked. No matter what their specialty, inventory, or pricing, keep a list of them because all yards will at some time or another have a part that you need.

New car dealers are another source of parts. They deal exclusively in new parts, and if you are looking for current replacement parts you will find them an ideal source. They stock (or can order) any recent sheet metal body component, primed and ready to paint. New car dealers will stock parts (or readily obtain them) for cars (usually) up to five years old. For cars more than seven years old, the salvage yard is the best body part source. Always check price with new part dealers. Remember that they get premium prices for their wares in order to establish the inventories they maintain.

A highly recommended source is Mill Supply (Tabco). Mill Supply features an infinite inventory of new component panel parts for most cars, and can provide steel panel and fender parts for over 50 different makes, foreign included. Their metal quality is high and you can count on them for hard-to-find and older car components, all at reasonable prices.

Mill will ship UPS or truck and will accept VISA or MasterCard. An illustrated catalog is available from this supplier for $2.00. Catalog orders or inquiries should be forwarded to:

Mill Supply Inc.
3241 Superior Avenue
Cleveland, Ohio 44114
(216) 241-5072

PAINT, BODY SHOP SUPPLIERS, AND TOOLS

Your local auto supply shop (*bodywork*, not mechanical) will usually be able to provide you with fillers, sandpaper, fiberglass, paint, thinners, primers, spray guns, and bodywork air tools.

Paint of the types mentioned in Chapter 18 is manufactured by five or so major manufacturers. All are good; some are favored by individual painters because of isolated characteristics. For the weekend painter I recommend the R-M and Ditzler Brands: in lacquer, R-M's Alpha-Cryl or Ditzler's Duracryle; in enamel (urethane), R-M's Super Max or Ditzler's Delstar. The neophyte painter should confine himself to using lacquer only as it is easier to spray and manipulate.

For information on the R-M and Ditzler paint lines, write to:

Rinshed-Mason Products
Inmont Corp.
Detroit, Michigan 48210

Ditzler Automotive Finishes
PPG Industries
Box 3510
Troy, Michigan 48084

Big body shop gear (air compressors) can be rented if you are on a budget or can be obtained reasonably from sources such as Sears or Montgomery Ward.

Specialized bodywork air tools are found at the same auto body suppliers that stock paint and other bodywork sundries.

A good and readily available source for special tooling is Snap-On. The Snap-On Tools headquarters is in the midwest but they have a door-to-door (or rather, shop-to-shop) sales network and local Snap-On salesmen are readily accessible to the average tool shopper.

The Snap-On trucks usually make their rounds to body and mechanical shops in a localized area. If you can locate the Snap-On salesman's route in your immediate vicinity (garage, body shop, etc.), you can meet him on a subsequent visit to study and select tools from his large inventory or special-order a tool to be delivered the next time around. You can get a current Snap-On Tool catalog from the route man or order one from:

Snap-On Tools
2801 80th St.
Kenosha WI. 53140

Snap-On offers not only an infinite variety but also quality and superior tooling.

Glossary

acetylene: Volatile gas used in conjunction with oxygen for gas welding.

acrylic enamel: Improved enamel medium superior to alkyd enamels; contains urethane and acrylic additives and catalysts.

acrylic lacquer: A lacquer-type fast-drying medium that relies on an acrylic plastic substance in its formulation for durability and gloss retention.

air compressor: A motor-operated machine with an integrated piston-type pumping mechanism for supplying air pressure to air tools and spray guns.

alignment: The correction of·panel or sectional spacing. Alignment is also applicable in front end and frame correction.

alignment gap: Space between panels in structural body of autos.

arcing: Moving the spray gun in an uneven arcing motion, resulting in uneven coatings.

atomization: The breaking up of paint into air-suspended particles using forced air transmitted and united with paint in the spray gun.

bleeding: The undercoat showing through new coats by contaminating and intermingling with overcoat film.

blistering: Surface bubbles appearing in paint coats due to contamination, dirt, or moisture.

blushing: Chalking or dull casting on freshly applied paint due to condensation of moisture or improper balance of thinner and atmospheric humidity conditions.

buckles: High spots associated with dents in sheet metal.

bumping hammer: Also known as *body hammer*. Used for rough shaping and pounding of damaged sheet metal.

catalyst (or hardener): A hardening chemical additive for plastic body fillers and some automotive paints.

cfm: Air measurement factor referring to *cubic feet per minute*.

"cheese grater:" File for forming newly applied body filler.

clear: A paint or paint overcoating containing no pigment.

compound: Polishing agent used to rub out acrylic and enamel finishes to a high luster.

cowl panel: Front auto body panel that retains and attaches to fenders, hood, and dash.

crazing: Small cracks in paint film caused by improper or imbalanced thinning or overabundance of paint film build-up.

curing time: The period of elapsed time necessary for the paint film to achieve its full strength and adhesion stage through chemical action.

DA: Dual action rotary sander-grinder air tool.

disk grinder: A rotating power tool for grinding bodywork and metal and removing paint.

dollies: Anvil-like steel pieces used in conjunction with body hammers to straighten dents.

drip check: Viscous liquid substance for sealing and lining cracks and joints.

dry sanding: Sanding by means of dry and open coat papers not requiring water.

174

dry spray: Dull, imperfect coating due to premature solvent evaporation.

dry time: Period required in order for solvent to evaporate from paint coating.

elasticity: Flexibility of a substance or material.

enamel: Original, oldest type of automotive paint, not frequently used, which dries in two stages: first by solvent evaporation, then by paint film hardening.

epoxy resin: The basic medium used in conjunction with fiberglass cloth for repairing fiberglass panels and components.

extractor: Water trap unit inserted in compressor air lines to withdraw water and condensation forming in air tanks and hoses.

featheredging: Tapering and blending edge of broken areas or peripheral areas of paint or plastic.

fiberglass cloth: Spun glass woven material used in fiberglass repair.

fish eyes: Round, crater-like surface depressions in paint films due to oil and silicone contamination.

flash time: Period in which paint coating is dry to the touch but not yet fully cured.

glazing putty: An overly viscous priming medium used basically for filling in heavy scratches.

gloss: Surface shine or luster.

grit: Size measurement of sandpaper, governed by the size of abrasive particles.

hammer-off-dolly: Metal straightening method in which the dolly is held off-center of the hammer blow.

humidity: Amount of moisture in the air.

impact tool: A tool providing air-driven hammering (or rotating) action for cutting metal, breaking seams, and removing nuts and bolts.

lacquer: A quick-drying paint type that dries by evaporation.

lifting: The lifting or wrinkling of a paint coat caused by use of improper or incompatible paint overcoating systems.

masking: The covering of areas on vehicles not to be painted in order to control overspraying.

metal conditioner: A rust-inhibiting chemical applied to bare metal prior to priming.

metallics: Lacquers or enamels containing suspended metallic particles in the pigment.

mist coat: An application of paint that is thinned and applied lightly.

orange peel: Paint finish with the appearance of the pebbly surface of an orange; caused by applying paint that is not adequately thinned.

orbital sanders: Power tools that fine-sand by means of an oscillating action (DA or Jitterbug).

overspray: Overextension of spray pattern falling on adjacent areas.

oxidation: Combined action of air and paint in which oxygen in the air causes a chemical action to take place. This is the basic drying and curing action aligned to basic enamel.

paint adhesion: The ability of the paint to cling to its under-surface. It is promoted by good and proper surface preparation.

paint film holdout: The ability of a paint film to resist penetration of a newly applied topcoat.

pick hammer: Metal bodywork hammer with one blunt side and one long, pointed side.

pinholes: Small holes or pockmarks in paint films or body filler coats. Can be caused by trapped air or moisture.

plastic body filler: A puttylike, heavy, viscous compound for filling irregularities and depressions in reformed metal surfaces to bring the surface to an equal and even level. Also known as *Bondo*.

prime coat: An application of primer or primer/surfacer, usually to a prepainted or bare metal finish. Assists in promoting good adhesion and filling in minor surface imperfections.

reducer: A name given to enamel solvent.

resin: Medium used in fiberglass repair.

respirator: A mask for housing inorganic or organic filters. Highly recommended for painting with hazardous materials such as acrylic enamel and acrylic lacquer.

retarder: A solvent additive that slows down the evaporation and drying time of the paint film.

rocker panels: Narrow panel areas located under car doors.

sags and runs: Caused by the film slipping of paint due to overthinning or overapplication of paint.

sand scratches: Prominent scratching in paint or metal caused by using too-coarse a grit of sandpaper.

sealer: A protective liquid medium used to coat a painted surface prior to repainting in order to diminish the possibility of poor adhesion, lifting, or bleed-through.

siphon-type spray gun: A spray gun that draws and atomizes paint by means of a vacuum caused by the rapid flow of air within in a siphoning action.

solids: The substances in paint solutions that form the paint coat.

solvent: Thinning medium added to paint in order to thin down the consistency for proper spray application.

spot putty: See *glazing putty.*

spray gun: Tool for atomizing and applying paint.

stripping: Removing paint films by applying chemical solvents.

tack rag: A cheesecloth-like rag dipped in a solution to make it sticky. It is primarily for picking up dirt and dust from a surface prior to painting.

thinner: Solvent for lacquer and acrylics.

toxic fumes: Associated with paints and some auto body filling mediums; can affect eyes, skin, and lungs.

triggering: Manipulating the air-paint flow of the spraygun.

trim: Metal decor pieces on car, including chromework and moldings.

twist damage: Distortion to crossmembers of automobile frame.

unibody construction: Auto construction in which the body and frame are an integrated unit.

viscosity: The consistency or "body" of a liquid, or its thickness.

welding: The joining and fusing of metals by melting them by gas or electrical means.

wet coat: A heavy application of paint.

wet sanding: Sanding with "wet" paper and water.

wrinkling: Paint film imperfection caused by exposure to heat or incompatible solvents.

Index

179

Edited by Steven H. Mesner

Popular Science Book Club offers a wood identification kit that includes 30 samples of cabinet woods. For details on ordering, please write: Popular Science Book Club, Member Services, P.O. Box 2033, Latham, N.Y. 12111.